Mission San Luis Rey

Father Antonio Peyri,
founder of Mission San Luis Rey.

Mission San Luis Rey

AN ILLUSTRATED HISTORY

by

Harry Kelsey

LIBER APERTUS PRESS

Revised edition published 2016; first published 2003.

Liber Apertus Press
P.O. Box 6226
Oceanside, CA 92052-6226
www.liberapertus.com

ISBN 978-0-9785881-2-0

For my favorite children

Mark, Joseph, Edward, Mary Jeanne
Martha, Matthew, Jane, Sarah

Contents

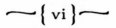

Illustrations

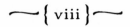

—{ x }—

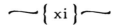

Acknowledgments

"May Honor be given to whom Honor may be due."

Samuel Adams

No historian works alone. Rather, he depends on antiquarians, archivists, librarians, and others who are determined to preserve records of the past. They deserve whatever faint honor comes their way.

First among them is Father Evan Howard, O.F.M., former guardian of the mission. He welcomed me to the mission and made all the mission records available for my use. Mary Whelan, Ed Gabarra, Robert Whelan, and Father Michael Gagnon, O.F.M. were equally cordial and helpful.

Among the archival and library collections, the following were most useful: The Santa Barbara Mission Archive and Library; the Archives of the Archdiocese of Los Angeles; and the collections of my own institution, the Huntington Library.

More recently Julie Ferraro, director of the Mission San Luis Rey Museum, suggested numerous corrections and revisions of the text. Beyond that, my daughter Martha Oven, and my son Matthew Kelsey worked very hard to see that the text was both accurate and clearly written. Should anyone find errors that they have overlooked, I may very well try to blame others, though I hereby absolve these three of any responsibility.

Harry Kelsey

Introduction

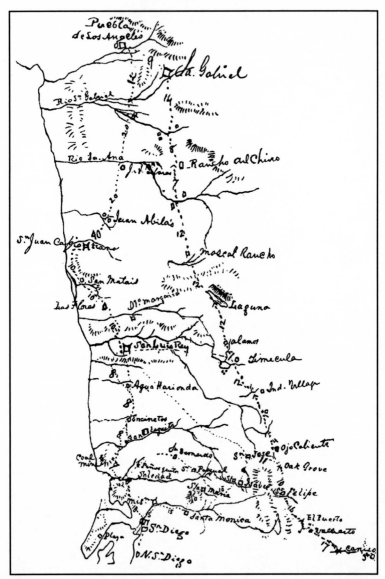

Map of Southern California missions and settlements drawn in 1850 by Lt. Cave Johnson Couts of the 1st Dragoons, U.S. Army.

In the sixteenth century mind, all the vast expanses of the New World were available to Europeans by right of discovery, so long as the lands were not governed by some other Christian ruler. With this sort of concept, it was not necessary for Europeans to think of the frontier as an area of vacant wilderness, as nineteenth century Americans did. Any populated region whose lands did not belong to another Christian prince was open to discovery and occupation. And the newly-conquered people were then obliged to become loyal and productive servants of the crown.

Just emerging from several centuries of war and conquest on the Iberian peninsula, Spain was uniquely equipped for expansion into the New World. Over time the Spanish government had managed to create a system of frontier institutions working more or less in harmony to assimilate newly annexed territories. These institutions were the presidio, the pueblo, and the mission. The presidio was a fortification, with a small cadre of regular army troops that could be augmented from the local populace in times of crisis. The pueblo was a town built around a plaza that served as the center of civil government and religious activity; both farmers and tradesmen had their homes here. The mission was a religious center, with the primary function of converting the pagan inhabitants to the Catholic religion and a secondary

responsibility for training these new Christians —
neophytes— to be productive citizens. This dual operation
was the purpose of Mission San Luis Rey.[1]

[1]For more on the Spanish settlement system see Oakah
L. Jones, *Los Paisanos: Spanish Settlers on the Northern
Frontier of New Spain* (Norman: University of Oklahoma
Press, 1979), 3-15, 206-208. The interaction of the mission,
presidio and civil community is also described in the
foreword by Donald C. Cutter and the remarks by the
author, Gilbert R. Cruz, in *Let There Be Towns: Spanish
Municipal Origins in the American Southwest, 1610-1810*
(College Station, TX: Texas A & M University Press,
1988), xi-xiii, 109-10, 201. A good summary of the special
role of the mission in Spanish frontier policy is found in
John F. Bannon, *The Spanish Borderlands Frontier, 1513-
1821* (New York: Holt, Rinehart & Winston, 1970), 59-63,
234-36.

1
The Natural Setting

Vischer's view of the mission ruins in 1865

L ocated on a grassy knoll on the south bank of the San Luis Rey River about three miles from the Pacific Ocean, Mission San Luis Rey was one of three missions in the Southern California Coastal Range. San Luis Rey occupies a wide valley cut from the granitic soil of a marine terrace. Before settlement, there were groves of sycamores, alders, and willows along the streams and in the river basin, with stands of grass and thick brush in the bottom lands, oak trees on the surrounding hills, and thick groves of pine at the higher elevations.[1]

It is not possible to know with certainty what the natural vegetation was before the arrival of the earliest settlers, but it is surely true to say that nearly everything is different now. Man has manipulated the environment as far into the past as we can delve with any certainty. When Juan Rodríguez Cabrillo sailed along this coast during the first week of October 1542, he saw a land of rolling hills and

[1] Rocco Louis Gentilcore, "Missions and Mission Lands of Alta California," *Annals of the Association of American Geographers* (March 1961), 51:49-53. Richard L. Carrico, "Cultural Resource Test Sampling Program for a Proposed Flood Control Project in the Lower San Luis Rey River Drainage, Oceanside, California," Report to the U.S. Army Corps of Engineers, Los Angeles District (October 1979), 1-5. Michael J. Moratto, *California Archaeology* (Orlando, Fl: Academic Press, Inc., 1984), 116-17.

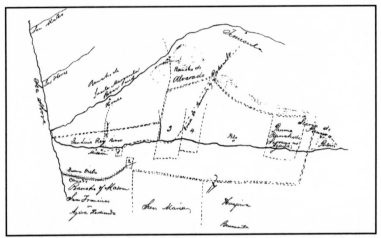

Map of San Luis Rey and surrounding village-ranchos from the
William Carey Jones claim of 1853.

grassy fields, with high mountains in the background. It
was a beautiful country, but dense clouds of smoke hung
over everything, a result of the Indian practice of setting
fire to the fields. This annual conflagration increased the
yield of seed-producing grasses and other plants that
provided forage for small game animals. Both plants and
animals were food for the Indians, but the fires also
destroyed brush and trees that prevented erosion of the
hillsides.[2] Even so, the stands of native pines were thick
enough in 1798 that within a month of the establishment of
the mission, several roof beams, a few *vigas* or crossbeams,
and two or three hundred pieces of construction timber
were cut from nearby forests and hauled to the building

[2] Harry Kelsey, *Juan Rodríguez Cabrillo* (San Marino, CA: Huntington
Library, 1986), 152-53, 159.

Ford drawing of the mission garden.

site.[3] Some sources, relying on an earlier translation, have the military construction crew cutting and hauling 175 roof beams in the first month, a nearly impossible job for such a small detachment.[4]

[3] Fermín Francisco de Lasuén to Miguel Lull, 20 June 1798, in Finbar Kenneally, *Writings of Fermín Francisco de Lasuén* (Washington, DC: Academy of American Franciscan History, 1965), 2:89-90.

[4] The problem is in the translation of *morillos*, which Kenneally properly renders as framing material. See Zephyrin Engelhardt, *San Luis Rey Mission* (San Francisco, CA: James H. Barry Co., 1921), 12, citing a letter

(continued...)

Although there was little or no agriculture before
the arrival of the Spanish soldiers, settlers, and
missionaries,[5] this future mission site contained relatively
large areas of level land suitable for farming. In some ways
San Luis Rey was in a much better location than either of
its companion missions, San Diego to the south and San
Juan Capistrano to the north, although none of the sites was
considered to be especially fertile.[6] George Vancouver,
visiting the region in 1792, remarked on the fertile soils at
San Juan Capistrano, and presumably at the river of San
Luis Rey.[7] The missionaries had noted the same: there was
reasonably fertile soil, an ample supply of timber, and

(...continued)
from Lasuén to Diego de Borica, 27 July 1798. A Spanish historian
thought the word ought to signify building stone, Lázaro Lamadrid
Jiménez, *El Alaves Fray Fermín Francisco de Lasuén, O.F.M.* (1736-
1803) (Vitoria: Diputación Foral de Alava, Consejo de Cultura, 1963),
277, note 878. Erosion could even be a blessing, as fish and waterfowl
thrived in the silt of marshes and coastal lagoons. Moratto, *California
Archaeology*, 116.

[5] Some authorities argue for a sort of "proto-agriculture" during the
prehispanic period. See Lowell J. Bean and Harry Lawton, "Some
Explanations for the Rise of Cultural Complexity in Native California with
Comments on Proto-Agriculture and Agriculture," in Lowell J. Bean and
Thomas C. Blackburn (eds.), *Native Californians: A Theoretical
Retrospective* (Socorro NM: Ballena Press, 1976), 19-48.

[6] Gentilcore, "Missions and Mission Lands of Alta California," 49, 53.

[7] George Vancouver, mentions increasingly barren soil from San Diego
southward, and from this Gentilcore infers an occasional alkalinity in the
soil near San Luis Rey. *Ibid.* The best modern edition in which to consult
Vancouver's description of the coastal region is the four volume edition
edited by W. Kaye Lamb, *A Voyage of Discovery to the North Pacific
Ocean and Round the World, 1791-1795* (London: Hakluyt Society,
1984), 1125-26.

running water. Perhaps the deciding element in identifying this valley as a future mission site was the fact that the Indians, who spoke the same language as those at Capistrano, told the missionaries they would become Christians, if a mission were established nearby.[8]

[8] Juan Mariner, diary, 26 August 1795, Archives of Santa Barbara, Bancroft Library, Berkeley, CA, quoted in Engelhardt, *San Juan Capistrano Mission*, 5.

2

The Prehistoric Era

A young Luiseño named Pablo Tac made this drawing of native costumes in the 1830's.

History began in the San Luis Rey valley in early October 1542, when Juan Rodríguez Cabrillo sailed along the coast and recorded what he saw. Everything earlier is prehistory, and those earlier "records" are interpreted by archaeological and paleontological analysis. Specialists used to say that people migrated to the New World from eastern Asia by way of the Bering Land Bridge, but others argue for different routes and other origins.[1] Some radio carbon tests have been construed to mean that the continent was inhabited thirty or forty thousand years ago, or even earlier. A skull found at Del Mar, thirty miles south of San Luis Rey, was assigned an age of 48,000 years, based on amino-acid racemization tests. However, there is a dispute about the age of the specimen used to establish the chronological formula, and there is considerable disagreement about the general reliability of amino-acid dates. Authorities do agree that human habitation in the San Luis Rey River

---

[1] R. Bonnichsen and A. L. Schneider, "The Battle of the Bones," *The Sciences* (July-August 2000), 40:40-46. K. Garrett, "The Hunt for the First Americans," *National Geographic* (December 2000), 198:40-67. C. L. Malcolm, "The Color of Bones," *New York Times Magazine* (2 April 2000), 40-45.

valley began at least twelve thousand years ago. Earlier dates have not yet been confirmed to everyone's satisfaction.[2]

Archaeologists also agree on three cultural traditions in the prehistory of this region: San Dieguito, which began about 9,000 years ago; La Jolla, with an inception date somewhat earlier than 7,500 years ago; and Late Prehistoric, including the San Luis Rey Complex, immediately preceding the mission period.

The best known example of the San Dieguito cultural tradition was found at a site called Rancho Park North, southwest of Batiquitos Lagoon. Lacking milling stones, these people subsisted on fish and shellfish, as well as local plants and small game. They had scrapers, blades, and knives of sharpened stone; they doubtless shaped handles and shafts from wood; and they probably made cordage from yucca fibers. But we know them only by these few remains, and no one is sure what happened to them. Perhaps they were forced out by La Jollan neighbors, but it is also possible that they developed a more complex way of life through their own initiative.[3]

What is certain is that the more sophisticated La Jolla cultural tradition replaced San Dieguito at Rancho Park North about 7,200 years ago. Basin-shaped milling stones and curiously contrived cogstones say something about the patient artistry of these people as well as their more elaborate methods of food gathering and preparation. Burial patterns make it possible to speculate about religious beliefs and

[2] Moratto, *California Archaeology*, 30-33, 49-51.
[3] Moratto, *California Archaeology*, 105-107.

practices, but not with any degree of certainty.[4] Closer to Escondido there is a cluster of archaeological sites known as the Pauma Complex, involving many elements of the La Jollan cultural tradition with some traces of San Dieguito. Not yet fully investigated or understood, the Pauma Complex is generally considered to be an inland variant of the coastal La Jollan cultural tradition.[5] The more distinctive elements of the Late Prehistoric traditions are found in the San Luis Rey culture, which has been generally dated at about 1400 to 1750 A.D. As the lagoons silted up, there was a pronounced shift to land-based food gathering. The food supply was vastly enlarged when someone discovered how to make acorns palatable. The process involved grinding the acorns in stone mortars, leaching out the bitter acidic components in sand basins, and cooking the finished product in baskets or pots. Perhaps as early as 1200 A.D. pottery was introduced to the San Luis Rey culture, introducing new possibilities for cooking and storing food, and demonstrating an even more sophisticated approach to daily life.[6]

---

[4] Moratto, *California Archaeology*, 148-51.

[5] Delbert L. True, "An Early Complex in San Diego County," American Antiquity (January 1958), 23:255-57, 262. True, "Archaeological Sites in San Diego County, California: Preliminary Report on Sites SDi-4558, 4562, and 4562A," Report to the California Department of Transportation, 1977, 6. True, "The Pauma Complex in Northern San Diego County: 1978," Journal of New World Archaeology (No. 4, 1980), 3:34-37.

[6] Clement W. Meighan named the earlier period San Luis Rey I and the later San Luis Rey II. See his article, "A Late Complex in Southern California Prehistory," *Southwestern Journal of Anthropology* (Summer 1954), 10:222. B. E. McCown, "Temeku: A Page from the History of the Luiseño Indians," *Papers of the Archaeological Survey Association of Southern California* (No. 3, 1955). True, Meighan, and H. Crew,

(continued...)

The first European expedition to visit this region was that of Juan Rodríguez Cabrillo in the fall of 1542. His ships were in the area for six months, and possibly he visited the villages near San Luis Rey, though no description of such an event has survived. The expedition of Sebastián Vizcaíno passed very close to the coast line on November 20, 1602. Excited at the size of the ships and perhaps remembering gifts from earlier visitors, the Indians signaled for the sailors to land. The fleet attempted to anchor at San Juan Bay but failed to find shelter and sailed on to Catalina Island. What the visitors might have found is known only by inference. At Catalina Island the explorers discovered children with blonde hair and white skins, a genetic gift from some earlier expedition, perhaps that of Cabrillo or Drake or Cermeño.[7] Cabrillo left a description of a village further up the coast in the Santa Barbara Channel that might well describe San Luis Rey at the time of first contact. The people lived in round dwellings made of reeds tied to a wooden framework. In the center of each village was a great plaza, surrounded by a plank fence and a stone curbing. Inside the enclosure were large wooden posts covered with religious symbols. Food consisted of seeds, nuts,fruits, fish, and game. In the summer time the people were well fed and happy; in the middle of winter, food was scarce, and the inhabitants were not at all hospitable. People painted their bodies and decorated themselves with beads and

[6](...continued)
"Archaeological Investigations at Molpa, San Diego County, California," *University of California Publications in Anthropology* (1974), 11:93-97.
[7] See "Father Antonio de la Ascension's Account of the Voyage of Sebastian Vizcaino," in Henry R. Wagner, *Spanish Voyages to the Northwest Coast of America in the Sixteenth Century* (San Francisco: California Historical Society, 1929), 237.

small weapons of stone and bone and shell. Feathers placed here and there in the hair added additional color. Clothing was almost nonexistent, except for capes of elk or bearskin, worn by important chiefs. There is no archaeological data to confirm the type of premission architecture in San Luis Rey territory.[8] This is not exactly what the first visitors to the San Luis Rey valley reported in 1769, but it is near enough to make us understand what the villages looked like and how the people lived in the early eighteenth century.[9]

Each village consisted of one or more "parties" or powerful families, each party led by a hereditary chief and attracting smaller groups with no chief. Each village occupied its own recognized territory, with associated hunting and gathering regions. This village organization remained largely intact after the arrival of the missionaries.[10]

Along with their Late Prehistoric neighbors, the San Luis Rey people cremated their dead and buried the remains in ceramic jars. One of their most distinctive new developments was a unique geometric style of rock painting. Diamond chains, zig zags, and similar shapes were typical. Some of the designs seem to have been related to observances like the

---

[8]See Delbert L. True, Clement W. Meighan, and Harvey Crew, "Archaeological Investigations at Molpa, San Diego County, California," *University of California Publications in Anthropology* (1974), 11:75.

[9] Kelsey, *Juan Rodríguez Cabrillo,* 152-53, 159.

[10] The basic works on the Luiseño social system are Edward W. Gifford, "Clans and Moieties in Southern California," *University of California Publications in American Archaeology and Ethnology* [*UCPAAE*] (No. 2, 1918), 14:155-202; William D. Strong, "Aboriginal Society in Southern California," *UCPAAE* (No. 1, 1929), 26:1-358; and Raymond C. White, "Luiseño Social Organization," *UCPAAE* (No. 2, 1963), 48:91-194.

girls' puberty ceremony, but other purposes were also involved.[11]

The complicated religious system of the San Luis Rey people has been described in great detail by Gerónimo Boscana. This scholarly Franciscan lived at San Luis Rey mission and had his information at first hand. Trying to describe the religion of the people in the time before the missions were established, he wrote about a system called Chinigchinich in which religious knowledge and power were nearly one and the same. The village chief was a religious leader as well, though there were others who had charge of important hunting and gathering activities and rituals.[12]

Probably it is unnecessary to say that the good father was not an admirer of the Indian religious system or of pagan patterns of behavior. But he was an acute observer, and nearly everything we know about Luiseño religion in the Late Prehistoric period is from his account. When he tells us that the Indians "in the end deceive us at every turn," he was probably referring to the very real element of fear in the Chinigchinich system. Years later, after a century of Christianization, Indians were still afraid to say much about the old religion.[13]

[11] Ken Hedges, "Hakataya Figurines from Southern California," *Pacific Coast Archaeological Society Quarterly* (No. 3, 1973), 9:1-40.

[12] Gerónimo Boscana, "Memoria breve de las costumbres gentilicas de los Yndios de San Juan Capistrano," in Henry and Paule Reichlen, "Le Manuscrit Boscana de la Bibliothèque Nationale de Paris: Relation sur les Indiens Acâgchemem de la Mission de San Juan Capistrano, Californie," *Journal de la Société des Américanistes* (1971), 15:242, 245-46, 254-60.

[13] Constance G. Dubois, "The Religion of the Luiseño Indians of Southern California," *University of California Publications in American Archaeology and Ethnology* (No 3, 1908), 8:76.

Viva Jesus.

Relacion historica de la creencia, usos, costumbres, y estravagancias de los Indios de esta Mission de S. Juan Capistrano, llamada la Nacion, Acagchemem.

Introduccion.

El haverme determinado a escrivir esta historia fabulosa en si, o en lo que contiene; pero verdadera respeto de estos Indios ha sido primeramente para poder dar, en algo cumplimiento a mis obligaciones de Misionero Apostolico, teniendolo siempre presente, y la mira, como tambien dejar a mis venideros instruccion y luces para que puedan governarse sin tanto trabajo como a mi me ha costado, procurando por todos modos, empleando todos los medios posibles para adquirir el conocimiento de la creencia, uso y costumbres que tenian estos naturales en su gentilidad, y por la misericordia de Dios con trabajo y maña en el espacio de mas de diez, años, he podido averiguar con una moral certidumbre todo quanto en el presente escrito se refiere.

Y estar persuadido de que ignorando la creencia que tienen los Indios, en sus usos, y costumbres, es muy dificil sacarlos del error en que viven, y darle a entender la verdadera Religion, y enseñarles el verdadero camino para su salvacion. Confieso que es dificil poder penetrar sus secretos, porque el significado de sus usos, y costumbres no lo saben todos, esto es solo para los Capitanes y algunos Sabajas, que hacian el oficio de Sacerdotes, y pregoneros, y quando estos lo enseñavan a sus hijos (y esto solo a los que los havian de suceder) era siempre con la advertencia que no lo manifestaran a nadie, porque si lo decian ó manifestavan tendrian muchas desgracias, y que se moririan ó infundiendoles mucho temor y miedo y por tanto se sabe tanpoco de sus cosas, porque los pocos que lo saben y entienden lo tienen reservado para si.

CHINIGCHINICH;

A

HISTORICAL ACCOUNT

OF THE

ORIGIN, CUSTOMS, AND TRADITIONS

OF THE INDIANS AT THE MISSIONARY ESTABLISHMENT

OF ST. JUAN CAPISTRANO, ALTA CALIFORNIA;

CALLED

THE ACAGCHEMEM NATION;

COLLECTED WITH THE GREATEST CARE, FROM THE MOST INTELLIGENT
AND BEST INSTRUCTED IN THE MATTER.

BY THE

REVEREND FATHER FRIAR GERONIMO BOSCANA,

OF THE ORDER OF SAINT FRANCISCO,

APOSTOLIC MISSIONARY AT SAID MISSION.

TRANSLATED FROM

THE ORIGINAL SPANISH MANUSCRIPT,

BY ONE WHO WAS MANY YEARS A RESIDENT

OF ALTA CALIFORNIA.

NEW YORK:
PUBLISHED BY WILEY & PUTNAM,
No. 161 BROADWAY.

1846.

In the succession of cultures from San Dieguito to San Luis Rey, there was a pattern of increasing sophistication in food gathering and preparation. As might be expected, this produced a marked improvement in the health of the people. One indication of this is the significant decrease in periods of malnutrition in the Late Prehistoric era. This does not mean that starvation periods ended, simply that they decreased in frequency and duration. This is clear from a study of skeletal remains.

Periodic starvation results in the formation of radiopaque transverse lines or bone scars on the femur. In tests on the skeletons of 102 adults from the population of prehistoric California incidence of transverse lines was found to be most frequent in the earliest period, less frequent in the middle period, and least frequent in the Late Prehistoric period. The conclusion is that the periods of starvation decreased as the subsistence level improved.[14]

Similar skeletal evidence has been used to study the prevalence of disease in prehistoric times. In California this approach is hampered to some extent by the Late Prehistoric practice of cremating remains of the dead, but there are sufficient data to show that health conditions here were probably not greatly different from those elsewhere in the Southwest. There is a persistent myth that Indians lived a basically healthy, happy, and peaceful existence, prior to the arrival of Europeans. The facts give a somewhat different picture of conditions in the region in the Late Prehistoric

---

[14] Henry McHenry, "Transverse Lines in Long Bones of Prehistoric California Indians," *American Journal of Physical Anthropology* (July 1968), 29:1-18.

period.[15] For example, a skeleton found near the campus of the University of California at Irvine and carbon-dated at 1560 A.D. (+/- 140 years) bears evidence that the individual probably suffered a violent death "by blunt instrument and projectile with the remote possibility of decapitation." The femur of this same individual bears a lesion that may indicate a fracture and subsequent infection. Vertebral flattening and lipping is interpreted as an indication of either arthritic degeneration or a back injury. The teeth are badly worn from gritty material deposited in the food during the grinding process; there is also some tooth loss, pyorrhea, and two small cavities, though fluoride from marine food sources may have retarded tooth decay.[16] The possible beneficial effect of marine fluoride has been noted elsewhere. [17]

The list of diseases and afflictions prevalent in the region in Late Prehistoric times is just about what might be expected in a region of growing village populations. As villages increased in size, so did the opportunity for the spread of infectious disease. Streptococcal and staphylococcal infections were common, as were gastrointestinal diseases

---

[15] Charles F. Merbs, "Patterns of Health and Sickness in the Precontact Southwest," in David H. Thomas (ed.), *Columbian Consequences: Archaeological and Historical Perspectives on the Spanish Borderlands West* (Washington: Smithsonian Institution Press, 1989), 41-42.

[16] Henry C. Koerper and E. Bonita Fouste, "An Interesting Late Prehistoric Burial from CA-ORA-119-A," *Pacific Coast Archaeological Society Quarterly* (April 1977), 13:39-61.

[17] See for example, Eric W. Ritter and Peter D. Schulz, "Mortuary Practices and Health Conditions among a Small Prehistoric Population from Baja California Sur," *Pacific Coast Archaeological Society Quarterly* (January 1975), 11:43-53.

associated with drinking contaminated water. The debate about the existence of certain diseases in prehistoric California continues, but skeletal evidence seems to indicate that tuberculosis and venereal syphilis were present prior to contact with Europeans.[18]

One of the major problems in the identification of prehistoric pathogens is the difficulty in diagnosis. Tuberculosis, for example, was long thought not to have existed in prehistoric North America because skeletal evidence had not yet been discovered. But in a medically unsophisticated population, infected individuals are likely to die at the first onslaught of the disease, before skeletal change can take place. Even so, the disease has been identified in most parts of prehistoric North America. There is a similar problem with coccidioidomycosis. Also called valley fever, this disease has so many of the same symptoms as tuberculosis and syphilis that it was not even recognized as a

---

[18] Jerome S. Cybulski reviews the pertinent evidence for syphilis in his article, "Possible Pre-Columbian Treponematosis on Santa Rosa Island, California," *Canadian Review of Physical Anthropology* (Nos. 1 & 2, 1980), 2: 19-25. Walker *et al.* note the existence of "treponematosis," but fail to recognize that this is a reference to syphilitic infections. In a curious analysis of similar material, Roy Salls noted a typical "crater-like lesion" on a skull but concluded that it could not be syphilis, unless the carbon dating was wrong and the skeleton was historic rather than prehistoric. See his paper, "Skeletal Remains from the Ripper's Cove Site, Santa Catalina Island, California," *Pacific Coast Archaeological Society Quarterly* (1984), 20:26-27. Signs both of tuberculosis and of venereal syphilis have been found in prehistoric skeletal remains in other parts of the Southwest, as is clear from Merbs, "Patterns of Health and Sickness in the Precontact Southwest," *Columbian Consequences*, 49-50.

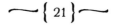

separate disease until 1894. It is now generally agreed that this disease also was endemic in Prehistoric California.[19] Disease itself was poorly understood. People often tended to look at sickness as a result of witchcraft or spells cast by enemies, and this may have been an important reason for going to war. Another reason was the introduction of the bow and arrow, a new technology that made it possible to kill or injure an enemy without being in close personal combat. In some parts of Southern California warfare became so widespread and so violent in the Late Prehistoric period that entire villages were destroyed and regional populations were decimated.[20] Whatever the cause, death came early in prehistoric California. Few people lived beyond the age of 25 or 30. In one sample from Catalina Island, seventy-seven percent of the adults over 15 years of age died before the age of 33. Infant mortality is difficult to determine for this era, but it was also very high.[21]

This should not be taken to indicate that life in California was worse than life elsewhere. The available evidence seems to indicate that the prehistoric people who lived in the San Luis Rey river basin were very much like people elsewhere in the world, especially the hunter-gatherer groups. They were

---

[19] Helmut Kloos, "Valley Fever (*Coccidioidomycosis*): Changing Concepts of a 'California Disease,'" *Southern California Quarterly* (Spring 1973), 55:59-88.

[20] Phillip L. Walker, Patricia Lambert, and Michael J. DeNiro, "The Effects of European Contact on the Health of Alta California Indians," in Thomas (ed.), *Columbian Consequences,* 355-56, 359-60.

[21] Clement W. Meighan, "Indians and California Missions," *Southern California Quarterly* (Fall 1987), 69:194.

often happy, but there were periods of trouble. Food was usually adequate, but often it was in short supply. Children died young, and most people did not live beyond the age of forty. Summers were the happiest times, and winters were difficult. Religious beliefs placed close constraints on the lives of the people, though religious knowledge was the province of specialists and most people did not know much about it. There were brutal wars, and violence was too often a familiar occurrence. In other words, they faced problems similar to those people faced elsewhere, and they struggled to find solutions.

Man of San Luis Rey and woman of Monterey

3

Founding the Mission

View of the mission by William Rich Hutton, 1849.

The first recorded visit to the San Luis Rey river valley came on Tuesday, 18 July 1769. Responding to international events, plus a desire to expand the northern frontier of New Spain, the Spanish government had dispatched a Sacred Expedition to establish military garrisons and Indian missions in Upper California. The first elements of this group arrived in San Diego in April, and by mid July a party, including Fray Juan Crespí, began to march overland to find Monterey Bay.

After a few days of travel, they arrived at "a large and beautiful valley, so green that it seemed to us that it had been planted." This was the San Luis Rey valley, which Fray Juan called San Juan Capistrano and marked as the site of a future mission. There was no running stream in the river bed, but there were several large ponds in the middle of the valley and a village at each end. There was good pasture for the horses, and grapes grew in such profusion that some places seemed almost like vineyards.[1]

There are two stories about the expedition's arrival, one Spanish, the other Indian. According to Fray Juan Crespí, the Spanish party made camp, and forty or so of the local men came to meet them, their flesh adorned with the many-hued paintings that were customary on important occasions and when going to war. The chief addressed the soldiers and friars, then all the men threw their bows and arrows on the ground, perhaps as a sign of peace. Gifts were exchanged: Spanish beads for some nets of agave fiber. The friars and the Indians got on well, and this was true throughout the trip.[2]

The Indian story was written between 1834 and 1841 by Pablo Tac, an Indian boy from San Luis Rey who studied in Rome to be a Franciscan priest. The Indians, according to Pablo's story, sat down and watched the Spanish for awhile, then the village captain got up, approached the newcomers, and demanded: "What are you looking for here? Get out of our country!" But the Spanish did not understand what he was

---

[1] Juan Crespí, diary, 18 July 1769, translation in Herbert E. Bolton (ed.), *Fray Juan Crespí, Missionary Explorer non the Pacific Coast, 1769-1774* (Berkeley: University of California Press, 1927), 129-31. The original manuscript of the diary does not survive. Bolton took his version from copies appearing in Fray Francisco Palóu's *Noticia de la Nueva California* and a manuscript copy of the diary made by Fray Francisco García Figueroa, as he explains in his introduction, p. lxii.
[2] Juan Crespí, diary, 18 July 1769, in Bolton (ed.), *Fray Juan Crespí*, 129-31.

saying, and the Franciscan began to talk to the people. The priest gave them gifts, the village chief was won over, and they all became friends.[3]

There are a few glimpses of pre-contact Luiseño life in the priest's diary. Friar Juan remarked on an area just to the north where the Indians had set fires in order to drive rabbits into their traps. Two days later they were at a village where a double tragedy was unfolding: one small child was horribly burned and on the point of death, while another sick child was dying at its mother's breast.[4]

Despite the friendly demeanor of the local people, it was nearly twenty years before a mission was founded there, sites to the north and south receiving preference. Mission San

---

[3] Pablo Tac, "Conversión de los San Luiseños de la Alta California," fol. 80, microfilm MS 255, roll 3, Huntington Library, San Marino, CA. The original manuscript is in the Biblioteca dellárchiginnasio di Bologna. It has been edited and published, somewhat carelessly, by Carlo Tagliavini in "L'Evangelizzazione e i Costumi degli Indi Luiseños secondo la Narrazione di un Chierico Indigeno," *Proceedings of the Twenty-third International Congress of Americanists* (1930), 638-39. There is a useful English translation by Minna and Gordon Hewes, *Indian Life at Mission San Luis Rey* (San Luis Rey, CA: Old Mission, 1958). Both these editions neglect to mention that the manuscript is really a disjointed set of historical notes, interspersed with the beginnings of a grammar and dictionary. Pablo Tac seems to have prepared a plan of the mission, keyed to part of his text, but this has disappeared.

[4] Juan Crespí, diary, 20-22 July 1769, in Bolton (ed.), *Fray Juan Crespí*, 132-35.

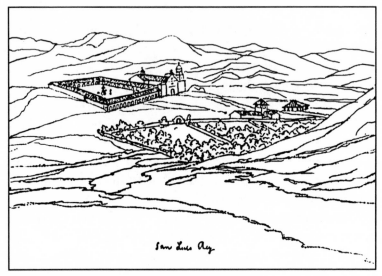

The mission in 1850, drawn by H. M. T. Powell.

Diego was started by Junípero Serra just two days before the explorers arrived at the Luiseño village. And when Mission San Juan Capistrano was built in 1775-78, it was placed at a site thirty miles to the north. Not until 13 June 1798 were the Franciscans able to start the mission, which was given the name of San Luís Rey de Francia.

Records of the time are confusing, but it seems clear that the site chosen for the new mission was a hilltop near the village of Tacayme, though Pablo Tac recalls that the people called the area Quechla, the Indian name for the stone found here. When the priests returned, the Indians gave them a warm welcome and asked them to stay. His story of the

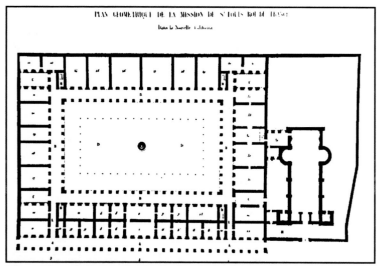

Plan of the mission copied by Duflot de Mofras from the original master plan.

arrival, written decades later and apparently based in part on information from Father Peyri, is different from the report written at the time by the priests who founded the mission. "Before the arrival of the Franciscans," said Pablo Tac, "our country was a grove of trees, but the Franciscan Father ordered us to cut them and in this way create a meadow." The Franciscans, for their part, reported that there were trees nearby, but not a large forest. In any case, the trees were cut, near the village and at some distance away, and made into roof beams and lumber. Stones were hauled to the site by Indians and by the soldiers as well. There had been a problem at San Juan Capistrano, where the soldiers refused to help construct the mission buildings. This time they had orders from the governor to work without murmuring. Some of the San Luis Rey people had been working at Santa Barbara, and other trained workers were sent from Missions San Diego and San Juan Capistrano.

Father Antonio Peyri, who was at the mission from the time it was founded until the time of secularization, seems to have followed a definite building plan. There was little of the constant tearing down, shifting about, and rebuilding that went on at other missions. It is possible that there was even a set of master drawings to guide the work. The illustrations published in 1844 by the French traveler Duflot de Mofras have the look of such drawings and may have been copied from a master set at the mission. Whether this is so or not, we know that the great mission quadrangle was erected rapidly, room by room and wing by wing, with such precision that it could scarcely have come about by chance.

The first buildings were shelters made of poles and brush "in the Indian fashion," one a temporary chapel, the other a house for the priests, both built just a day or two before the founding of the mission.[5] The experienced construction

---

[5] Father Peyri told the visitor Auguste Bernard Duhaut-Cilly in 1827 that the first buildings were some huts built in the Indian fashion, plus a place to say Mass in the morning. See his *Voyage autour du Monde Principalmente a la Californie* (Paris: A. Bertrand, 1834-35), 2:50-51. There is a useful translation of the pertinent portions by Charles Franklin

crews managed to have a few adobe rooms finished by the end of the year, space for the padres, the soldiers, and the corporal of the guard and his family. Houses for both girls and boys, a weaving room, and some store rooms were added the following year. In 1800 the permanent guardhouse was built, with rooms for the corporal and all of the soldiers.[6]

Up to this time the roofs had been made of tules or brush and earth, called *terrado*. In 1801 the mission work crews began producing roofing tile, and half of the roofs were changed in that year. Probably in the first year an adobe building was constructed for use as a church. Remodeled but still too small, it was replaced by a larger, tile-roofed church in 1802, perhaps at the eastern end of the north wing. All the other mission buildings were re-roofed with tile. Granaries, shops, and storerooms were added in succeeding years, as well as two brick tanks for tanning hides, and a large brick boiler for making soap.[7]

By the end of the year 1804, the several wings of the mission had been extended to form a quadrangle,[8] with large gates in the middle of the north and south wings, leading to an interior patio measuring about 250 by 280 feet.[9] In 1806 new

---

Carter in the *California Historical Quarterly* (June 1929), 8:131-65.

[6] Engelhardt, *San Luis Rey*, 9-16.

[7] Bancroft, *History of California*, 2:107-108. Engelhardt, *San Luis Rey*, 18.

[8] Engelhardt, *San Luis Rey Mission*, 18.

[9] Father Engelhardt reports that he and Father Jeremiah O'Keefe measured the interior of the patio and found it to be 250 feet square. See his *San*

quarters with a private patio were built for the girls and unmarried women. According to the annual report, this patio was 26 by 16 *varas*,[10] which is exactly the size of the small patio that used to be at the at the southwest corner of the complex.[11]

The gardens northwest and south of the mission were enclosed in adobe walls, and brick bathing and laundry facilities were built around the springs in the lower garden. There was also construction work at more distant villages, where cattle and sheep ranches and farms were operated.[12]

Luis Rey Mission, 18-19, 38. Henry L. Oak visited the mission in 1874, while all the walls were still standing or visible. He made detailed measurements and a ground plan, which show the patio to have inside dimensions of 84 by 93 yards. The drawing can be seen in his journal, "A Visit to the Missions of Southern California in February and March 1874," MS 564, Braun Memorial Library, Southwest Museum, Los Angeles. The journal, including a somewhat dim reproduction of the ground plan, was published in Ruth F. Axe, Edwin H. Carpenter, and Norman Neuerburg, *A Visit to the Missions of Southern California in February and March 1874, by Henry L. Oak* (Los Angeles: Southwest Museum, 1981), 30.

[10] Engelhardt, *San Luis Rey Mission*, 19. A *vara* is about 33 inches.

[11] Oak, "A Visit to the Missions of Southern California," MS 564, Southwest Museum. Duhaut-Cilly described a separate courtyard for the girls and unmarried women. See his *Voyage autour du Monde*, 2:52. Tac recalled a similar courtyard for the boys. See his "Conversión de los San Luiseños de la Alta California," fol. 84v, microfilm MS 255, roll 3, Huntington Library.

[12] Engelhardt, *San Luis Rey*, 19.

The mission in 1827, with an Indian village
southeast of the quadrangle.

For example, the attractively designed quadrangle at Las
Flores was built in 1823.[13]

In 1811 the priests hired a carpenter and mason named
José Antonio Ramírez and began to draw up plans and lay the
foundations for a new church, the fourth on the site. An
arched portico was begun inside the main patio, and a new
wing was added to the main buildings of the quadrangle,

---

[13] Annual Report, San Luis Rey Mission, 31 December 1823, Santa
Barbara Mission Archive, microfilm MS 42, Huntington Library.

perhaps the wing that extended to the north and east.[14] The carpenter-mason may be the man Duhaut-Cilly calls "un homme fort ingenieux." By 1815 the new church was completed, and the building was dedicated in October of that year.[15]

For the most part the Indians lived in their usual manner at San Luis Rey, dwelling in round, conical huts, though some built more permanent houses. The main village at San Luis Rey seems to have been north of the mission buildings and close to the river, but some families lived elsewhere. Duhaut-Cilly said the Indian rancheria was located "to the north, two hundred paces from the mission," but the drawing published in his book shows the Indian huts on the east side of the mission buildings. The village is similarly located in the drawing published by Duflot de Mofras, though these may simply be the result of artistic attempts to balance the pictures and to show that Indians lived close to the mission. Most of the reports by other visitors say the village was located north of the mission compound but that dwellings were scattered all around the site.[16]

---

[14] Engelhardt, *San Luis Rey*, 34. Edith Buckland Webb, *Indian Life at the Old Missions* (Los Angeles: Warren F. Lewis, Publ., 1952), 130.

[15] Annual Report, San Luis Rey Mission, 31 December 1815, Santa Barbara Mission Archive, microfilm MS 42, Huntington Library.

[16] Duhaut-Cilly, *Voyage autour du Monde*, 2:55. Eugène Duflot de Mofras, *Exploration du Territoire de L'Oregon, des California et de la Mer Vermeille* (2 vols. in 4; Paris: Arthus Bertrand, 1844), 1:264. In an interview on 1 September 1932, Cave Couts, Jr., told Edith Buckland

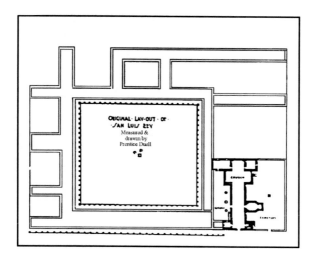

Ground plan of the completed mission by Prentice Duell.

Webb that the Indian village was north of the mission on both sides of the river. He thought the remains of the village might still be found. Webb Collection, Vol. XVIII, Santa Barbara Mission Archives.

4

Mission Life

Page from the San Luis Rey baptismal register, signed by Father Peyri.

There is no dependable estimate of population before the mission was founded. Numerous people have written about this matter, and the varying results furnish an interesting look at the methods historical statisticians use in their work. The most knowledgeable estimate of Luiseño population was that given by Pablo Tac in the 1830s. Reporting what was probably Father Peyri's appraisal of native population in 1798, this young Indian wrote: "Not long ago in Quechla and the surrounding countryside there were 5,000 souls, but two thousand died of an illness that came to California, and three thousand remained."[1] Since we know that the mission population when Pablo Tac left San Luis Rey was a little less than 3,000, it is possible to accept his estimate of the earlier population with a great degree of confidence.[2]

However, not everyone agrees with his assessment. Anthropologist Raymond C. White started with Tac's 1798

[1] Tac, "*Conversión de los San Luiseños de la Alta California*," fol. 92, microfilm MS 255, roll 4, Huntington Library.
[2] Annual report, San Luis Rey Mission, 31 December 1832, Santa Barbara Mission Archive, Santa Barbara, CA, microfilm, MS Film 42, at the Huntington Library, San Marino, CA.

In Pablo Tac's drawing the Luiseño dancer wears a net skirt and carries a bone rattle.

San Luiseño.

figures, but decided that it was "not unreasonable" to conclude that another two thousand people had died between 1769 and 1798, so there were really seven thousand living in the region of San Luis Rey when the "Sacred Expedition" arrived.[3] A curiously low figure is given by Sherburne F. Cook, who arrived at his conclusion in an unusually convoluted way. First, he took the total number of baptisms at the mission between 1798 and 1832, then subtracted the number of those born at the mission, and arrived at what he

[3]Raymond C. White, "Luiseño Social Organization," *University of California Publications in American Archaeology and Ethnology* (1963), 48:118-19.

considered to be the total number of "gentile" Indians baptized during the thirty-four year period. Cook then decided on an arbitrary "ratio of gentile baptisms to aboriginal population," which he set at 2:3 for the northern missions, 1:2.4 for the central group, and 3:4 for the five southern missions. With a total of 3,088 gentile baptisms at San Luis Rey, the aboriginal population would have been somewhat more than 4,000 in 1769.[4] If Cook's guess is correct, the population of the San Luis Rey region increased by 25% between 1769 and 1798. But if White is correct, just the opposite occurred, and the population decreased by nearly 30%! Obviously, the best that can be said with certainty is that there were about 5,000 Indians in the region in 1798. If there were only 3,000 converts during the next three decades, then many did not become Christians.

---

[4] Sherburne F. Cook, *The Population of the California Indians, 1769-1970* (Berkeley: University of California Press, 1976), 40-41. Many historians question Cook's methods and results. See, for example, David Henige, "On the Contact Population of Hispaniola: History as Higher Mathematics," *Hispanic American Historical Review* (May 1978), 58:217-37. See also Harry Kelsey, "European Impact on the California Indians," in Antonine Tibesar (ed.), *Junípero Serra and the Northwestern Mexican Frontier, 1750-1825* (Washington, DC: Academy of American Franciscan History, 1985), 82-84. In any case, Cook had no formal training, either in history or in anthropology. His field was physiology. Because of disputes about his work in his own field, Cook began to write in the field of ethnohistory, often with other faculty colleagues, such as Woodrow Borah and Robert Heizer. See Gloria R. Lothrop, "*El Viejo*: Serra in Context," *The Californians* (November-December 1989), 7:23.

This is one of the great anomalies of the mission period. Only a fraction of the Indian population joined the missions. Many were attracted to the life at the missions, the dependable food supply, and the ability to learn the language and customs of these obviously powerful strangers. By all accounts Father Peyri was a kind and loving pastor, attracting many Indians who disliked the fear-laden religion of Chinigchinich. But some were never converted, perhaps because they did not want to abandon the easy indolence of the hunter-gatherer life.

In any case, life at San Luis Rey did not involve a complete rejection of old customs. Father Peyri thought it better to have the Indians continue to enjoy their own dances and songs and to live in their own villages. There were several ranches and farms scattered around the mission, some having their own chapels where the missionary came every week or so to say Mass. Chapels were located at San Antonio de Pala about twenty miles to the east; Temecula, about thirty miles away in a northeasterly direction; and Las Flores, or San Pedro, about eight miles to the north. San Jacinto, to the northeast, had permanent buildings but may not have had a chapel. There were smaller farms and ranches at San Marcos to the east; at Pauma, east of Pala; at Santa Margarita, three miles north of the mission; and Agua Hedionda (San Francisco) and Buena Vista a short distance to the south. In addition, there was a village of "gentile" Indians at Portrero, near Pauma, which

Rancho Las Flores, about 1850.

may have furnished workers for the farms and ranches from time to time.[5]

[5] Tac, "*Conversión de los San Luiseños de la Alta California,*" fol. 92, microfilm MS 255, roll 4, Huntington Library, lists only three main ranchos, Pala, Las Flores (Usva in his text), and Temecula. When Julio César talked to Thomas Savage in 1878 about "Cosas de Indios de California," he recalled seeing chapels at the same three places. MS C-D 109, fol. 2, Bancroft Library, Berkeley, CA; a translation by Nellie Van de Grift Sanchez is available in *Touring Topics* (November 1930), 22:42-43. Wilma L. Locke said the San Jacinto buildings included a chapel, which in 1949 served as the living room of the main house at Casa Loma Rancho. See her paper, "In Search of an Asistencia," MS C-I 13:2, typescript in the Bancroft Library. Part of her information is from Ruth M. Pico and Gertrude Pico Harrison, whom she interviewed October 31, 1949; MS C-I 13:1, Bancroft Library. Mrs. Locke's search for a fourth chapel seemingly arose from the statement in Duhaut-Cilly's *Voyage*

(continued...)

Each farm and ranch was supervised by a Spanish majordomo, though the people who lived nearby received their instructions from elected Indian leaders called *alcaldes*, each of whom had charge of several villages. Every afternoon the alcaldes went to the mission for a meeting with the missionary and the "general," who was chief of the alcaldes and lived at the mission, as did the majordomos of the nearby ranchos. Every evening the alcaldes returned to their villages with news of the day and sometimes with special instructions for the next day's work.[6] The majordomos and alcaldes of distant ranchos came to the mission only once a week.[7] Though lacking his traditional authority, the village chief or "captain" still retained his ceremonial importance, greeted visitors, and wore a military coat and a plumed hat.[8]

---

[5](...continued)
1949; MS C-I 13:1, Bancroft Library. Mrs. Locke's search for a fourth chapel seemingly arose from the statement in Duhaut-Cilly's *Voyage autour du Monde*, 2:56, that there were four main ranchos, each with its own majordomo, village, and chapel. The locations of the various ranches are shown on the map annexed to the deposition of Juan Foster in the claim of William C. Jones to the lands of San Luis Rey Mission, 30 December 1853, 339 SD, Bancroft Library.

[6] Tac, "*Conversión de los San Luiseños de la Alta California*," fols. 65v-65, microfilm MS 255, roll 3, Huntington Library.

[7] Duhaut-Cilly, *Voyage autour du Monde*, 2:56.

[8] Tac, "*Conversión de los San Luiseños de la Alta California*," fol. 92v, microfilm MS 255, Roll 4, Huntington Library. The coat and hat are described in John R. Bartlett, *Personal Narrative of Exploration and Incidents in Texas, New Mexico, California, Sonora, and Chihuahua* (New York: D. Appleton & Co., 1854), 92.

Describing his own family at San Luis Rey, Pablo said the day started with breakfast of a hot drink, plus meat and tortillas. Then the man of the house might go hunting with a bow and arrow or go out to gather wood. The mother would stay home to take care of cooking and other chores. Children remained at the mission, going to school, but young married men and women would work at trades and in farm or ranch work, the women at spinning, weaving, or sewing, the men at various tasks connected with the farms or ranches. At noon everyone came home for lunch, then they returned to their tasks until mid afternoon. There was another meal in the evening before all went to bed.[9]

Pablo's parents were not among the skilled craftsmen of the mission, but he described the various crafts: spinning, weaving, sewing, iron work, soap making, the winery, the oil press, plus milling, farming, ranching, gardening, brick making, lime burning, and carpentry; in short, all the things that were needed to run an institution caring for several thousand people.[10] Much of this work took place in and around the mission courtyard. In the center was a fountain from which fresh water flowed, available for use as needed for drinking, cooking, washing, and in the various occupations.

Even though there are numerous partial descriptions, several sketches of the buildings, hundreds of photographs,

[9]Pablo Tac, "*Conversión de los San Luiseños de la Alta California*," fols. 66-66v, microfilm MS 255, roll 3, Huntington Library.
[10] Pablo Tac, "*Conversión de los San Luiseños de la Alta California*," fols. 84-85, 66-66v, microfilm MS 255, roll 3, Huntington Library.

and at least two ground plans, it is difficult to know exactly how the mission buildings were arranged. The most detailed plan is that published by Duflot de Mofras in 1844, a decade after the mission was secularized. Both his plan and his drawing of the front of the mission look like the work of a professional draftsman, but they bear only a very general similarity to the building that was actually constructed. Possibly they were copied from a master plan made when the mission was founded but not followed in detail.[11] Some of the major errors in the drawings are: two towers on the church, rather than one; a walled courtyard in front of the church; omission of several wings on the north, east, and west sides; erroneous placement of shops and quarters in the north, east, and west sides of the quadrangle.

Fortunately, there are drawings made from an actual inspection of the building site. The most detailed plan was drawn by Henry L. Oak, when he and Hubert H. Bancroft visited the mission in February 1874.[12] The occasion was a research trip by Oak and Bancroft to gather information for a multi-volume history of California. Their observations differ in important respects from the small drawing on the survey of

[11] Duflot de Mofras, *Exploration du territoire de L'Oregon: Atlas* (Paris: Arthus Bertrand, 1844), plates 23 and 24.

[12] Henry L. Oak, "A Visit to the Missions of Southern California in February and March 1874," MS 564, Braun Memorial Library, Southwest Museum, Los Angeles.

the property made by Surveyor John G. Cleal for Archbishop Joseph Alemany in September 1854.[13]

But by comparing the various plans with the brief descriptions and the rough measurements given in the annual reports of the missionaries, it is possible to make some tentative identifications of some parts of the mission quadrangle and associated structures.

It seems appropriate to begin at the mission church, as nearly all the visitors have done. Duhaut-Cilly called this

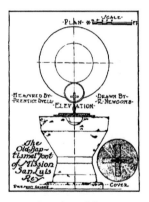

Baptismal font

[13] Results of the survey were entered as evidence in the bishop's claim for the property. Locations of the various records in this case are described by Harry B. Morrison in his article, "The Archbishop's Claim: The History of the Legal Claim of the Catholic Church before the Federal Courts to the Property of the California Missions," *The Jurist* (No.2, 1987), 47:394-422.

Sketch of the
main altar
after restoration.

building "a palace,"[14] and Bancroft said it was "unequaled in many respects by any structure in California today."[15] A tower on the east front held five bells in two tiers. The west tower was never completed, though the church was probably designed to have two towers, if the drawing by Duflot de Mofras is any guide. The main altar was backed by a gilded reredos, decorated with statues of various saints, including

[14] Duhaut-Cilly, *Voyage autour du Monde*, 2:47-48.
[15] Hubert H. Bancroft, "Personal Observations during a Tour of the Line of Missions of Upper California," Cal. MS. E113, Bancroft Library, Berkeley, CA.

San Luis Rey de Francia at the top and a wooden image of the Virgin Mary below. There were two side altars, the one on the right decorated with statues of San Joaquín and Santa Ana, parents of the Virgin, plus another statue of San José. The other side altar was dedicated to San Antonio.[16]

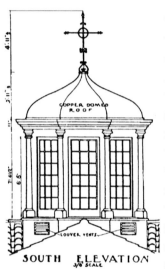

SOUTH ELEVATION
⅜" SCALE

There was a dome over the transept, illuminated by a cupola with 144 small panes of glass, designed, we are told, by Fray Antonio himself. It is possible that the glass-enclosed cupola was not added until 1829, though the dome itself was there when Duhaut-Cilly visited the mission in 1827.[17] The walls were of adobe with brick reinforcement and trim. The floor was cement, and the ceiling was made of wood. There were eighteen other windows, nine doors,[18] two choirs, and two

[16] Tac, *"Conversión de los San Luiseños de la Alta California,"* fols. 63-64, 84.

[17] Annual Report of Mission San Luis Rey, 31 December 1829, Santa Barbara Mission Archives, microfilm MS 42, reel 2, Huntington Library, San Marino, CA. Duhaut-Cilly, *Voyage autour du Monde*, 2:52.

[18] *"Inventario y avaluo general de los bienes de la Mision de Sn. Luis Rey formado por Fr. Buenaventura Fortuni y los Comisionados Pablo de la Portilla y Pio Pico,"* 22 August 1835, in Archives of California, State Papers, Missions, Tomo VI, fols. 11-12, Bancroft Library. There is a
(continued...)

sacristies, one of which may have served as a chapel for the infirmaries nearby.[19]

While the building was still under construction, an earthquake shook the entire coast of California, wrecking church buildings and creating considerable havoc at every mission, including nearby San Juan Capistrano, where a number of people were killed in the church. The greater portion of the damage at San Juan Capistrano was caused by the bell tower falling into the nave of the church. Fear of similar damage at San Luis Rey probably led to the decision to eliminate the stairway in the east bell tower and to fill the space with adobe brick. The west tower was left without a domed cupola. Instead, an outside stairway was built to the second floor of the east tower, giving access to the choir loft and then to the east tower.[20]

West of the church was a small garden, with fountains and fruit trees. Beyond this were the buildings of the main mission quadrangle. Separate infirmaries for men, women, and children occupied the south portion of the east wing,

[18](...continued)
typescript copy with a satisfactory translation of the document in the Owen C. Coy Collection, California State Library, Sacramento.

[19] Pablo Tac, "Conversión de los San Luiseños de la Alta California," fol. 84, microfilm MS 255, roll 3, Huntington Library.

[20] See the report on the Estado de las Misiones de la Alta California, 1812, Archivo de las Misiones, 1769-1856, MS C-C 4-5, file folder 525. Unfortunately no details are given for damage at San Luis Rey.

adjoining the garden. In order to make it easier for the sick to attend Mass, a special chapel was built for them, just down the corridor from the infirmaries and next to the main sacristy of the church.[21] After the mission was secularized, visitors who saw the ruins of this pretty little garden mistakenly concluded that it was built as a private garden for the priests.[22]

This wing also housed the wine cellar, which must have been an extremely large room, judging from the amount that was needed for Mass, for the dinner table of the Franciscan priests, and for sale to visitors. Pablo Tac said there were 200 *pipas* of wine, brandy and white wine, or 400 casks altogether, stored in this room. The wine press was in an adjoining room. Both these rooms were very likely in the southeast corner of the east wing, separated from the infirmaries by an open hallway leading to the small garden and the entrance to the church.[23]

---

[21] *Estado de las Misiones de la Alta California*, 1818, Archivo de las Misiones, 1769-1856, MS C-C 4-5, file folder 543, Bancroft Library. Sea also Duhaut-Cilly, *Voyage autour du Monde*, 2:52. See also the drawing by Duflot de Mofras, *Exploration du territoire de L'Oregon: Atlas*, plate 24.

[22] See, for example, the entry for 12 March 1850, H.M.T. Powell, Journal, 1:189, MS C-F 115, Bancroft Library, Berkeley, CA.

[23] Tac, "*Conversión de los San Luiseños de la Alta California*," fol. 75, 84, microfilm MS 255, roll 3, Huntington Library. Duflot de Mofras, *Exploration du Territoire de L'Oregon: Atlas*, Plate 24. Both Tac in his description and Duflot de Mofras in his plan locate the winery and cellar in the same place, facing south between the church and the rooms of the Franciscans.

The south wing contained a double row of rooms, generally for the use of the missionaries and official visitors.[24] In the center of this wing was a parlor or reception room for important visitors. An upright clock standing in one corner of this room, doubtless worked at one time but was inoperative before the mission was secularized. There were oil paintings hanging on the walls in the parlor, and some of the walls in this section were decorated with murals as well. Furnishings and chairs were about what might be expected in such an establishment: large pieces made of wood with leather upholstery. The south wing had colonnades on both sides, with a few glass or shuttered windows, and doors leading out of each room. One small door was intended for use as an emergency escape route in case of earthquake. One of the most interesting structures was the kitchen, whose massive chimney was topped by an attractive lattice-work of brick.[25]

The colonnade along the south front of the mission contained thirty-two arches, each about fourteen feet on center. However, the interior courtyard was much smaller than this, because the west wing started at about arch number twenty-five, and the inner court had 23 arches on the north and south sides, 21 on the east and west. The west wing

[24] Oak, "A Visit to the Missions of Southern California," ground plan. Duflot de Mofras, *Exploration du territoire de L'Oregon: Atlas*, plate 24.
[25] Tac, "*Conversión de los San Luiseños de la Alta California*," fol. 63v, 84v, microfilm MS 255, roll 3, Huntington Library. George W. Ames, Jr. (ed.), " A Doctor Comes to California: The Diary of John S. Griffin, Assistant Surgeon with Kearny's Dragoons, 1846-47," *California Historical Society Quarterly* (December 1942), 21:334.

housed the dormitories for the boys and young bachelors and separate dormitories for the girls and young maidens. Each of these dormitories consisted of several rooms built around its own courtyard. Pablo Tac reported that there were orange trees inside the courtyard of the boys' residence; presumably there were similar trees in the girls' courtyard as well.

The dimensions of the girls' courtyard were 26 by 16 *varas*, according to the 1806 annual report.[26] This is almost exactly the same as the courtyard shown at the southwest corner of the mission in the Oak drawing, 16 by 25 yards.[27] In fact, there is another courtyard of the same dimensions at the northwest corner, but which was for males and which for females is impossible to say. If Tac's description of the rooms surrounding the quadrangle follows a generally clockwise direction, as it seems to do, then the courtyard for the boys was at the southwest corner, and that for girls at the northwest corner. The square between these two courtyards may have been a corral or a storage yard for the wagons and carts.[28] The Hewes translation describes the dormitory for the boys as containing "a patio and two gardens (*plantas*)." However, the word *plantas* is used elsewhere in the manuscript (fol. 63v) to refer to *plantas de naranja*, and that is doubtless its meaning here.

[26] Engelhardt, *San Luis Rey Mission*, 19.
[27] Oak, "A Visit to the Missions of Southern California," ground plan, MS 564, Southwest Museum.
[28] Tac, "*Conversión de los San Luiseños de la Alta California*," fol. 84v, microfilm MS 255, roll 3, Huntington Library.

The remainder of the quadrangle housed the blacksmith shop, shoemaker's shop, the carpentry shop, the weaving room, school rooms, and similar places. A large L-shaped wing ran north and west from the north wing and probably housed storage rooms. Another wing running west from the west wing probably contained dwelling space for the various majordomos, the matrons, and the craftsmen whose work kept them close to the mission compound.[29]

Gracing the center of the quadrangle was a large "wooden clock" (*reloj de palo*). Though it sounds extraordinary now, clocks made mostly of wood were common in the early nineteenth century. It could have been made locally or purchased from a visiting trader. Apparently this curious machine did not survive secularization, as none of the later visitors mentioned having seen it.[30]

In front of the mission, on the south side, was the guardhouse, with quarters for both married and single soldiers, shown here in a drawing by H. M. T. Powell. A bit closer to the church was a large dwelling for the majordomo. Both of these structures are accurately portrayed in the drawing by Duhaut-Cilly.[31] About a hundred yards to the south was the

[29] Tac, "*Conversión de los San Luiseños de la Alta California*," fols. 75, 84v, microfilm MS 255, roll 3, Huntington Library.

[30] Tac, "*Conversión de los San Luiseños de la Alta California*," fols. 63v, 84v, microfilm MS 255, roll 3, Huntington Library.

[31] Duhaut-Cilly, *Voyage Autour du Monde*, 1:199. Both buildings were still usable when the U.S. Army occupied the mission during the Mexican War. See the drawing of the building by Cave J. Couts, MS CT 2542, and his journal, MS CT 2541, pp. 67-68, Huntington Library.

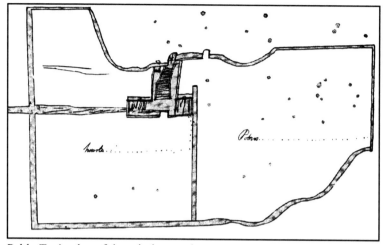

Pablo Tac's plan of the mission garden.

great garden of the mission. This was an imposing place, enclosed entirely by a wall, with an entrance flanked by pillars and an arched gateway. There was a turnstile in the gateway to keep horses and cattle away. Beyond this was a wide flight of tile steps leading down to tile basins constantly flushed with running water. Here the people obtained drinking water from two stone spouts made in the shape of gargoyles. Here too, the people bathed every morning, at least when the weather was pleasant. Later in the day, women returned to wash their clothes. The garden was divided in the middle by a wall. On the east side was a grassy meadow; on the west a gardener tended fruit trees (peaches, pears, apples, pomegranates) melons, and squash for the neophyte families, plus salad vegetables and herbs for the missionaries. The water flowed from the springs and pools in this garden, through a watergate, and down an irrigation channel to another garden where vegetables were grown for mission use. All told, there were three such gardens at San Luis Rey, plus two others at Pala and Santa Margarita.[32]

Soldiers quarters.

[32] Tac, "*Conversión de los San Luiseños de la Alta California*," fols. 86-87v, 90, microfilm MS 255, roll 4, Huntington Library. Julio Cesar, "Cosas de Indios de California," fols. 1-2, MS C-D 109, Bancroft Library, is authority for the statement that the other garden was at Santa Margarita. Tac said he could not remember where it was.

5

The End of
the Luiseño Mission

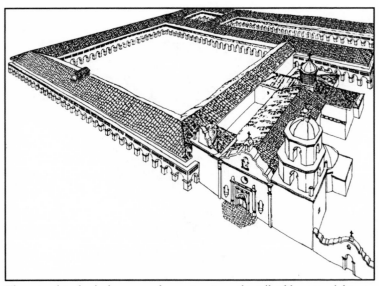

The completed mission was a huge structure, described by one visitor as the largest in California.

By 1830 the mission was well established, and the Luiseño people were prosperous and happy. Then everything changed. Under considerable pressure from local residents who coveted the Mission lands, the Mexican government issued a series of decrees, emancipating the Indians and announcing that the mission would be transferred to secular control. Father Peyri, who had been at the mission from the very start, quickly saw that secularization was simply a way to transfer former mission lands to the control of local landowners, without much regard for the rights of the Indians themselves. After enduring various trials, the priest received permission to retire in December 1831 and left the mission in January 1832. The mission then came under the control of various secular officials, generally not men of great probity.[1]

The most notable of the numerous administrators who made off with mission lands and property was Pio Pico. Appointed late in 1835,[2] Pico operated the mission properties

[1]These tragic events are detailed in Engelhardt, *San Luis Rey Mission*, 73-136.

[2] The exact date of appointment is unclear, but the date on the inventory which he signed on 22 August 1835 is probably very close to the time he took control. Archives of California, State Papers, Missions, Tomo VI, fols. 11-12, C-A 51, Bancroft Library.

Alfred Robinson sketched the Luiseño mission and village in 1829, just before the Franciscans were forced to leave.

as though they were his own and treated the Indians like slaves.[3] Along with his brother Andrés, he took possession of Las Flores and established his residence there, moving in with young girls from the Indian community and making

[3] Julio César called Pico a despot. See his "*Cosas de Indios de California*," MS C-D 109, pp. 4-5, Bancroft Library.

General Don Andres Pico of Los Angeles, 1868.
A Californian Magnate in his home.

the place a private seraglio.[4] But when he announced his intention to occupy the rancho at Temecula, the Indians determined to resist.[5] A new administrator, José Antonio Estudillo, was ultimately appointed to replace Pio Pico.

His appointment was doubtless effective about 16 August 1540, when he signed the inventory of mission property.[6] He, too, retired in possession of a mission ranch, San Jacinto. Julio César said that Estudillo took the ranch, the cattle, and everything.[7] In the end the Indians lost everything.

As the mission buildings deteriorated and the livestock and chattels disappeared, many of the Indians left the mission without formal emancipation, though they lacked real plans for supporting themselves. The main problem seems to have been an inability to work without the supervision of a chief (as in prehistoric times) or a missionary father (as in more recent days). When William Hartnell emancipated the Indians at Las Flores in 1839, he did not really believe that they could manage alone, partly because of interference from the Picos.[8]

[4] Francisco Ibárra to Narciso Durán, 7 May 1840, quoted in Engelhardt, *San Luis Rey Mission*, 114, fn. 14.

[5] Letter of Joaquín de los Rios y Ruíz, 15 March 1840, Archives of California, State Papers, Missions, Tomo X, fol. 262; and letter of William Hartnell, 26 August 1840, Archives of California, State Papers, Missions, Tom XI, fols. 9-10; C-A 51, Bancroft Library.

[6] MS 68/115:4, Bancroft Library.

[7] See his "*Cosas de Indios de California*," MS C-D 109, Bancroft Library.

[8] William E. Hartnell, diary, 31 May 1839, pp. 68-70, MS C-E 77:1, Bancroft Library; Hartnell, diary, 17 August 1839, MS C-E 77:5, Bancroft

(continued...)

Frustrated at their own repeated failure and angered by the oppression of the secular administrators, the Indians begged for the return of the padres, to oversee the operation of the mission lands.[9] For a time, after March 1843, the authority of the missionaries was enhanced somewhat,[10] but when Pio Pico became governor, much of the mission lands and property were sold to his brother José Antonio Pico and to Antonio José Cot.[11] Pico and Cot sold their claim in 1858 to William Carey Jones.[12] The District Court for the Southern District confirmed Jones' claim in 1861, but this decision was

[8](...continued)
Library; Hartnell, report, 24 June 1839, fol. 25, and report, 26 August 1840, fol. 11, Archives of California, State Papers, Missions, XI, C-A 51, Bancroft Library; letter from Pico to Hartnell, 5 June 1839, Archivo de las Misiones, Tomo 2, part 3, C-C 5 Phot., Bancroft Library. Bancroft, *History of California*, 3:346-49, 623-25.

[9] Letter from Pablo Apis *et al.*, 1 August 1838, Archives of California, State Papers, Missions, Tomo I, pp. 652-53, quoted in Engelhardt, *San Luis Rey Mission*, 104-105. This may be the only copy of the letter that survives. the Bancroft Library copy is only a one-line summary. See Archives of California, State Papers, Missions and Colonization, II, C-A 53, Bancroft Library. The original papers were destroyed in the 1906 fire in San Francisco, but Father Engelhardt made copies of many of the papers in 1904; *San Luis Rey Mission*, 19.

[10] Manuel Micheltorena to Francisco Arce, 26 March 1843, Santa Barbara Mission Archives, vol. VI, fols. 141-47, Papeles Miscelaneas, C-C 12, Bancroft Library.

[11]Decree dated 18 May 1846, typescript copy in Coy Collection, California State Library.

[12] See the deed dated 12 April 1858 in MS CT 1770, Huntington Library.

later reversed.[13] In any case, Rancho Santa Margarita was not part of the bargain, since Pio Pico kept that rancho for himself.[14]

Despite the difficulties that plagued his last years at the mission, San Luis Rey was in a flourishing condition when Father Peyri left in 1832. There were 2,788 Indians living at the mission and its various ranchos. Livestock herds included 27,500 cattle, 26,100 sheep, and 1950 horses. There were several large gardens, orchards, and vineyards. The children attended school, where they learned to read, to write, to play musical instruments, and to sing. The Indians loved the missionaries and depended on them for guidance.[15] Pablo Tac said of Father Peyri, "If anyone wants anything, he will ask the Missionary, who will immediately give him whatever he asks because he is the father of all."[16] Julio César, who did not know Father Peyri but knew his successor, Father Francisco

[13] U.S. District Court, Southern District of California, United States v. William Carey Jones, Case No. 339, 1 April 1861, MS CT 2333, Huntington Library. Engelhardt, *San Luis Rey Mission*, 135.

[14] Julio César says Pico paid for the rancho with 500 cattle taken from the mission herds. See his "Cosas de Indios de California," MS C-D 109, p. 3, Bancroft Library.

[15] Duflot de Mofras, *Exploration du territoire de L'Oregon*, 1:340-47. Alexander Forbes, *California: A History of Upper and Lower California* (London: Smith, Elder & Co., 1839), 230.

[16] Pablo Tac, "Conversión de los San Luiseños de la Alta California," fol. 86v, microfilm MS 255, roll 4, Huntington Library.

Ibarra, said that the Indians called him *Tequedeuma*, a Luiseño word that signified goodness and love.[17]

Nonetheless, it is impossible to judge just how the Indians fared in mission life. Without a doubt, the missions saved them from extermination. Many of them learned trades, married outside the mission, and were assimilated into the general population. But disease decimated their ranks, though it is impossible to know just how serious the problem was.[18] Syphilis and dysentery afflicted dozens at the mission, forcing the missionaries to build special hospitals to care for the sick.[19] These were abandoned when the missions themselves were disbanded.

No one knows what the mortality statistics might be for any of the missions. They are thought to be high, but no more so than for any similar population.[20] Mission population statistics provide only a few vague clues. The figures listed in the annual reports at San Luis Rey and other missions are nearly useless for statistical purposes. They list only baptisms, deaths, and present population, and there is no apparent correlation between the figures.

[17] Julio César, "Cosas de Indios de California," MS C-D 109, p. 1, Bancroft Library.

[18] The general pattern is described in Kelsey, "European Impact on the California Indians, 1530-1830," 504-511.

[19] "Estado de las Misiones de la Alta California," 1818, file folder 543, Archivo de las Misiones, 1769-1856, MS C-C 4-5, Bancroft Library.

[20] Meighan, "Indians and California Missions," 194. Sherburne F. Cook and Woodrow Borah, *Essays in Population History: Mexico and California* (3 vols.; Berkeley: University of California Press, 1979), 3:189-90.

It might be supposed that the number of baptisms less the number of deaths would equal the number actually living at the mission, but such is not the case. The actual population figure (*existentes*) is generally much different, and this is true at several other missions as well.[21] Birth rates may have been low, though this is unclear. The male population always outnumbered the female population at San Luis Rey, and it is not apparent why this should have been the case.[22] Nor is there any reason to suppose that the entire Luiseño population entered the mission by 1832. The inhabitants of at least one large village, Portrero, never joined the mission.[23]

[21] See the annual reports for San Luis Rey, 1800 to 1832, in the Santa Barbara Mission Archives, also on microfilm MS Film 42, Huntington Library. For an example of such comparisons at other missions see the "Estado que manifiesta el numero de indios," 1817, Archives of California, State Papers, Missions, IV, C-A 50, Bancroft Library.

[22] For example, in 1812 there were 778 males and 739 females at San Luis Rey; in 1818, 1157 males and 1059 females; in 1826, 1502 males and 1360 females; and in 1830, 1480 males and 1296 females. Archivos de las Misiones, 1796-1865, file folders 525, 543, 566, and 572, MS C-C 4-5, Bancroft Library.

[23] Julio César, "Cosas de Indios de California," MS C-D 109, p. 2, Bancroft Library.

6

The Mission in Ruins

While the palm tree remained
in the mission garden.
The gate that framed it
slowly collapsed.

Beset from all sides, the mission went into a rapid decline. By the time the U. S. troops arrived in California in 1846, the mission buildings were abandoned, and the Indian village nearby had declined drastically. John Bidwell, the first American administrator, found the Luiseños "friendly," "intelligent," and anxious to escape the servitude forced on them by the local population.[1] For a time the mission buildings served as barracks for the troops. The alcalde of the nearby village had the keys to the church, and the village people tried to protect the church and its contents.[2] Nonetheless, several Americans broke into the building and made off with some of the furnishings.[3]

[1] Quoted in Engelhardt, *San Luis Rey Mission*, 137.

[2] W. H. Emory, *Notes of a Military Reconnaissance from Fort Leavenworth, in Missouri, to San Diego in California, including Parts of the Arkansas, Del Norte, and Gila Rivers* (Washington: Wendell & Van Benthuysen Printer, 1848), 116. Emory says the village was a mile away, but Robert H. Whitworth says it was half a mile. See his diary, MS 68/91c, p. 101, Bancroft Library.

[3] Ames (ed.), "Diary of John S. Griffin," 346. Some local people tried to blame the Indians for loss of church property, but the Indians denied taking anything. Jonathan D. Stevenson to Richard B. Mason, 28 June 1847 and 12 July 1847, in Charles Hughes (ed.), "A Military View of San Diego in 1847," *The Journal of San Diego History* (Summer 1974), 20:36, 39. It seems unlikely in any case that the Indians would have stolen

(continued...)

San Luis Rey Upper California

View of San Luis Rey when soldier Robert Whitworth visited
the mission in 1847.

[3](...continued)
anything from the church. As some of them told Cave J. Couts, "to touch
anything connected with the Church . . . would be followed by an instant
stroke of death." See his journal, 10 April 1849, p. 67, MS CT 2541-1,
Huntington Library, San Marino, CA. This portion of the journal has been
edited by Thomas L. Scharf, "Pages from the Diary of Cave Johnson
Couts: San Diego in the Spring and Summer of 1849," *The Journal of San
Diego History* (Spring 1976), 22:9-19.

Women praying before the ruined altar.

The same thing happened in 1865, when U.S. troops were again quartered at the mission. An article in the *Daily Alta California* noted: "The altar and images were torn down by members of Detachment Co. E, 1st Cal., August 27th 1865. This detachment is under the command of Lieutenant Stow.

There were only four or five of the detachment engaged in this wicked conduct."

Edward Vischer made this drawing of the Luiseño village at San Luis Rey in early 1865.

Meanwhile, the Luiseño people slowly drifted away. When the census was taken in 1850, the Indian population at San Luis Rey was listed as 6. This doubtless means that the Luiseño population simply was not counted, but it was certainly very low in comparison to the population in 1832.[4]

[4] Probably as a result of having attended church services at the mission, members of the Visiting Committee to Examine Farms, Orchards, Vineyards, Nurseries, Mines, Mining, etc. for the State Agricultural Society reported in 1858 that there were "immense numbers of Indians" at San Luis Rey, many of whom were married to local Californios. See the *Transactions of the California State Agricultural Society during the Year 1858* (Sacramento: John O'Meara, State Printer, 1859), 279. However, the Indian alcalde at San Luis Rey told John Russell Bartlett in 1852 that of the 3,000 Indians who had lived at the mission and its dependencies twenty years earlier, only a few hundred remained "in some villages up the valley, a few miles from the mission." Bartlett, *Personal Narrative of*
(continued...)

In 1860, there were 108 Indians living in San Luis Rey Village, plus another 53 Indians living elsewhere in San Luis Rey Township.[5] Edward Vischer visited the Indian village in April and May 1865 and sketched the place as a tumble-down and nearly deserted village.[6] By 1870 there were only 25 Indians, all listed as servants, living in various dwellings in San Luis Rey Township.[7] Within a decade of secularization the Indians had been dispossessed from the mission, and in a short time they were forced out of the area altogether.

This was accomplished simply by opening the former mission lands to settlement and for the most part ignoring Indian claims to the land. Lacking a formal title from the Spanish and the Mexican governments and lacking the sophistication to take advantage of the U. S. land laws, the Luiseños failed to establish a tribal claim to the vast ranch lands once operated by the mission. Various private land claims dating from the 1840s were recognized, while the rest of the mission lands became public domain. One confused attempt to conclude a treaty with the Luiseños in 1852 was

---

[4](...continued)
Explorations, 2:92.

[5] U.S. Census, 1850, San Diego County, California, pp. 58-59, photostats in San Diego Historical Society Library. U. S. Census, 1860, San Luis Rey Township, San Diego County, California, dwellings 163-194, originals in San Diego Historical Society Library.

[6] His text is unclear, and he may have depicted a group of houses near the south garden. Edward Vischer, *Missions of Upper California, 1872* (San Francisco: Winterburn & Co., 1872), 38. See also his *Edward Vischer's Drawings of the California Missions, 1861-1878* (San Francisco: Book Club of California, 1982), facing p. 15, and plates 34-37.

[7] U. S. Census, 1870, San Luis Rey, San Diego County, p. 1, photostat in the San Diego Historical Society Library.

rejected by Congress, and it was late in the century before permanent reservations were established for the Luiseños.[8]

The ruined buildings continued to attract interest. At one point the state legislature attempted to convert the former mission buildings and surrounding land into a state university, but Archbishop Joseph S. Alemany entered a claim to the buildings, and the state university was located elsewhere.[9] The claim arose from information given to the archbishop by the Franciscan priests at Santa Barbara Mission. These missionary fathers had told Archbishop Alemany that all of the lands at the mission belonged to the Indians, "but that the Churches, Church edifices, stores, cemeteries, orchards, and vineyards with aqueducts should be considered the property of the Church."[10] Presumably, churches and support buildings were always intended for religious use, while stores, equipment, and furnishings purchased with money from the Pious Fund were similarly restricted. The same consideration applied to the vineyards, whose primary purpose was to raise

---

[8] Donald C. Cutter, "The La Jolla, Rincon, Pauma, Pala, and San Pasqual Indian Reservations in Historical Perspective," in Rincon Band, *et al.*, v. Escondido Mutual Water Company, *et al.* S.D. Cal. No. 69-217-S, pp. 26-56. Harry Kelsey, "The California Indian Treaty Myth," *Southern California Quarterly* (Fall, 1973), 15:225-238.

[9] "Notice of Commissioners of Seminary Lands forbidding settlers settling thereon," 30 November 1853. Copy in the Coy Collection, California State Library.

[10] Joseph Alemany, "Libro Borrador," p. 144, Archives of the Archdiocese of San Francisco, quoted in Morrison, "The Archbishop's Claim," p. 406. Bishop Alemany became archbishop of San Francisco in October 1853, while the claim was pending. Francis J. Weber, *Joseph Sadoc Alemany, Harbinger of a New Era* (Los Angeles: Dawson's Book Shop, 1973), 45.

grapes for Mass wine; and to the gardens, where food was grown for the priests.[11]

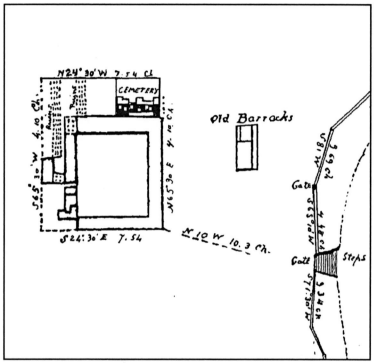

Map of the Mission of San Luis Rey by John G. Cleal, September 1854.

In order to support his claim, the archbishop hired John G. Cleal to survey the land occupied by the mission buildings and gardens, and this survey provides an interesting look at

---

[11] This was the custom in Europe. It is still the custom in rural Mexico for the parish priest to have land for chickens, a few pigs, a garden, and a cornfield, though Mass wine is usually available commercially now.

the condition of the mission property at mid century. His drawing of the garden south of the mission is very much like the drawing done by Pablo Tac, and easily identifiable in the ruined walls visible today. His drawing of the garden northwest of the mission is the earliest extant drawing of that important garden located near the Indian village. No doubt his exterior measurements of the main quadrangle and cemetery are accurate, but the interior of the mission is only a rough sketch, differing considerably from the measurements given by Bancroft, Bartlett, Oak, O'Keefe, and others who saw and recorded the ruins before they were removed. The exterior dimensions noted by Cleal are correct: 9.1 chains across the front, less 70 feet for the church and cemetery, which agrees exactly with the 530 foot measurement recorded by Bartlett in 1852; 7.54 chains north to south, which is the same as Bartlett's measurement, "upwards of six hundred feet." But the inner quadrangle was only about 300 feet square, leaving room for the unusually wide north wing and the separate courtyards for the children in the west wing.[12]

In any case, the mission was well on the way to ruin by the mid fifties. One of the northern corners of the quadrangle was

[12] On Cleal's plat, which is quite small (a 14" x 18" sheet), the tiny quadrangle is colored with a red wash and thus is indistinct. There are also some errors in measurement. For example, the distance between the quadrangle and the lower garden is about half what is listed on the plat. U.S. District Court, Northern District of California, Archbishop Joseph S. Alemany, Claimant, Mission Lands, Case No. 425 N.D., page 529, Bancroft Library. Bartlett, *Personal Narrative,* 89.

Edward Vischer's sketch of the buildings in May 1865 shows the entire north wing and much of the east wing roofless and in ruins.

falling to pieces when Bartlett and Cleal saw it,[13] while the northeastern extensions were already roofless and tumbling down. The roof of the church was in bad condition, some beams had collapsed in the front colonnade, and nearby farmers and ranchers were mining the buildings for brick, timber, tiles, doors, in fact anything that could be carted away.[14]

The destruction of this impressive structure became something of a scandal in the next decade. One visitor in 1862

---

[13] Cleal's plat shows the northeastern corner in ruins, while Bartlett said it was the northwestern corner that was falling down. U.S. District Court, Northern District of California, Case No. 425 N.D., p. 529, Bancroft Library. Bartlett, *Personal Narrative*, p. 89.
[14] Benjamin I. Hayes, Journal, 18 May 1860, "Emigrant Notes," part 3, p. 500; part 4, p. 525, MS C-E 62, Bancroft Library.

called it "a sort of quarry" for building materials.[15] A few soldiers, quartered there in 1865, stripped the main altar, probably for the gold ornamentation that had been placed there just a few years before the mission was secularized.[16] A traveler who saw the ruins in 1868 said, "Bishops, priests, and laymen are to be blamed." Father Mut, pastor at San Juan Capistrano, said most of the material was taken by local ranchers Foster and Couts, but they retorted that the priest himself had sold "a dozen pillars and arches" to "a squatter."[17] Finally, the new bishop, Thaddeus Amat, had a legal notice placed in the paper "to warn all persons not to take away the timbers, bricks, or other materials" from the mission.[18] A year later a similar report noted that "all of the buildings, except the church itself, and nearly all the corridors, [had] crumbled into ruins."[19]

When Henry Oak and his employer Hubert Howe Bancroft visited the mission in 1874 only six arches remained of the 32 that had graced the south front of the quadrangle. About half the rooms in the south wing, plus a few in the east and west wings, were still standing. Inside the church the

[15] John T. Doyle, "Introduction," to Francisco Palóu, *Noticias de la Nueva California Escritas por el Rev. Padre Fr. Francisco Palóu* (San Francisco: Imprenta de Edouardo Bosqui y Cia., 1874), xv-xvi.

[16] Letter from C.E.P., *Daily Alta California*, 24 November 1868, p. 2. Father Peyri reported the addition of gold ornamentation in his report of 31 December 1830, Santa Barbara Mission Archives, microfilm copy, MS Film 42, reel 2, Huntington Library.

[17] *Daily Alta California*, 24 November 1868, p. 2.

[18] Letter from Benjamin Hayes, Attorney, 10 October 1868, news clipping in Hayes, "Emigrant Notes," part 4, page 529, MS C-E 62, Bancroft Library.

[19] Letter from B.C.T. [Ben C. Truman], *Los Angeles Star*, 9 October 1869, news clipping, Hayes, "Mission Book," 1:159, Bancroft Library.

dome over the transept had cracked, so the parishioners had built a temporary wall of wood to seal this hazardous section from the nave of the church. The military quarters and the house of the majordomos, in front of the building, were in such a dilapidated condition that Oak could not tell exactly what sorts of buildings they had been.[20]

Sketch of the mission in 1856 by Henry Miller, showing Luiseño houses just above the quadrangle.

Bancroft, perhaps because of a question from his little daughter, Kate, noticed something that no one else remarked upon. "Surrounding the Mission buildings," he wrote, "were the usual irregularly placed out houses in which the Indians lived, some of them still standing."[21] These may be the small structures shown in Henry Miller's 1856 sketch of the mission, scattered mostly to the north and east of the main quadrangle.

[20] Oak, "A Visit to the Missions," MS 564, Southwest Museum.

[21] Bancroft, "Personal Observations during a Tour through the Line of Missions of Upper California," p. 69, Cal. MS E 113, Bancroft Library.

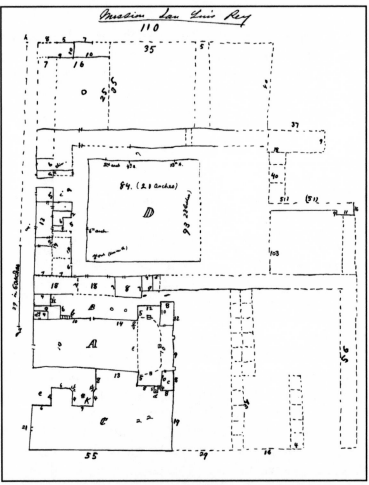

Henry Oak's mission plan contains detailed measurements of all the remaining ruins.

When Bancroft and Oak visited San Luis Rey, they found lodging in a little town adjoining the various remnants of mission property. The settlement was platted in September

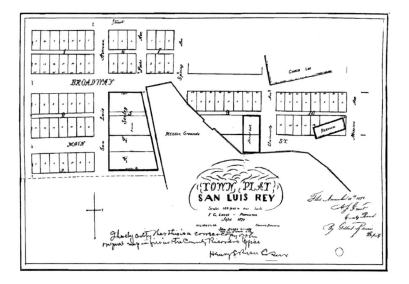

1871 as the Town of San Luis Rey, but local people insisted the name was Lockesville.[22] Most of the town lay west of the mission, between the two gardens, but an eastern extension took in part of the south front of the mission quadrangle.[23] It was not much of a town, according to Bancroft. The hotel was a "hovel," he said, "a small mud and board tenement with three beds in the front room, the floor of which was half covered with water." From the "filthy kitchen" came "greasy

[22] Robert E. Melbourne, "San Luis Rey in the Nineteenth Century: Its People, Institutions and Events," p. 109, M.A. thesis, University of San Diego, 1990.

[23] See the map in the San Diego County Plat Book, Township 11 South, Range 4 West, San Diego Historical Society. There is also a sketch map in Herbert Crouch, "Reminiscences," (1915), p. 19, typed MS C-D 5039, Bancroft Library. A similar manuscript, with map, is in MS 920 CRO, San Diego Historical Society.

and fish-like ham, stale stews, oak leaf-tea with no milk," and "third rate San Francisco store butter."[24]

Still, there were some of the marks of advancing civilization. Citizens of San Luis Rey in the 1870s could boast, if they felt like it, of having two cemeteries in addition to the one at the mission. The Pioneer Cemetery, of somewhat uncertain origins, is recognized in records dated 1875 and was doubtless intended for the use of persons not eligible for burial in the mission cemetery.[25] Within a decade there was another, All Saints Cemetery, adjoining the Episcopal church in the town of San Luis Rey.[26] Both of these cemeteries are still in use.

By this time the mission buildings were complete ruins. When Helen Hunt Jackson visited the mission in the early 1880s the south wing was unroofed, and the kitchen chimney towered all alone above the melted adobe walls. There had not been a resident priest since the last missionary died in 1846.

Even so, the church was standing, locked and guarded by the old Luiseño alcalde, who still lived nearby. The sacristy

---

[24] Bancroft, "Personal Observations during a Tour through the Line of Missions of Upper California," p. 35, Cal. MS E 113, Bancroft Library.

[25] Title Deed from Isaac M. Kolb to Edward J. Ripley, recorded 15 November 1875, Liber 26, San Diego County Recorder, copy in Oceanside City Planning Department files. See also the memo from Richard Ryals and Rita Baker to Richard Nagler, 12 January 1990, Oceanside City Planning Department files.

[26] See the "Map of All Saints Cemetery in San Luis Rey, San Diego County, California," MS CT 2599, Huntington Library, San Marino.

roof had fallen in, and the chapel domes on the east side had collapsed, but the main structure was still sound.[27]

The ruined mission kitchen, by Henry Sandham.

[27] Helen Hunt Jackson, "Father Junípero and His Work," *The Century Magazine* (June 1883), 26:202, 209, 214. See also the several photographs of the mission in c. 1875 (date established by Melbourne, "San Luis Rey in the Nineteenth Century," 119-121.

The alcalde in the mission church by Henry Sandham.

7

Return of the Franciscans

T hough the mission buildings were melting away, the town itself was beginning to prosper, and this may have been a factor in saving the mission church. Township population in 1886 was said to be 600, probably an exaggeration, but nonetheless indicative of a growing agricultural community.[1] The Catholic diocese owned some of the town lots, and the bishop was interested, in any case, in getting a resident priest into the area.[2] Consequently, in 1892, when Mexican Franciscans came looking for a place to establish a house of studies, he suggested they settle at San Luis Rey. The friars agreed, and on 10 July 1892, the bishop transferred the church property to the order, with the stipulation that an English speaking priest always be in residence to serve the Catholic people living nearby.[3]

[1] Douglas Gunn, *San Diego: Climate, Production, Resources, Topography, etc., etc.* (4th ed., rev; San Diego: Union Steam Book and Job Office, 1886), 16, 57. Gunn, *San Diego Illustrated: Climate, Resources, Topography, Productions, etc., etc.* (San Diego: San Diego Printing Co., 1887), 103.

[2] Plat of San Luis Rey Township, San Diego County plat books, San Diego Historical Society.

[3] See the Latin summary in John J. Cantwell to Bernard Klumper, 22 January 1922, Catholic Diocese of San Diego, archives. See also Francis J. Weber, *Francis Mora, Last of the Catalans* (Los Angeles: Westernlore Press, 1967), 22. There is additional information in [Finbar Kenneally],

(continued...)

Mission church and the ruined courtyard.

[3](...continued)
"San Luis Rey Golden Jubilee," *Provincial Annals* (January- April, 1955),
17:95-96. See also Isidoro Comacho to Guadalupe de Jesús Alva, 14
September 1893, quoted in Kean Tintle, "Mission San Luis Rey, 1893-
1900," p. 7, unpublished MS in the San Luis Rey Mission archives.

The Mexican friars and Archbishop Mora conducted their negotiations with the assistance of a friar from Santa Barbara Mission named Joseph Jeremiah O'Keefe. He immediately took up residence at the site to serve as local liaison and to help prepare living quarters for the priests and seminarians from Mexico.[4]

He decided to construct a temporary frame building facing the entrance to the church, perhaps incorporating an adobe structure that already stood on the site. This structure ultimately served as a kitchen, dining room, and chapel. Two other buildings appeared close by, the first a two-story wooden structure for living quarters, library, and classroom, and the second a storehouse, next to the kitchen.

The main work undertaken, however, was the restoration of the church. A new ceiling was installed, largely for protection of the congregation, and later an entirely new roof. Walls in the church were re-plastered after deteriorated

---

[4] Oceanside *Blade*, 1 January 1898, p.3, typescript in the San Luis Rey Mission archives. Valentine Healy, "Father O'Keefe, Rebuilder of Mission San Luis Rey," *Times Gone By: The Journal of San Diego History* (June 1965), 11:16-18.

adobes had been replaced by fired brick. The dome was
rebuilt, with a new lantern, and there were also new doors, a
new altar, and a concrete floor, poured over the original
floor.[5]

Probably there had always been an intention to rebuild the
quadrangle, and this work finally began in 1903. Much
smaller than the original quadrangle, the new structure

nonetheless was built on top of the old. Details are sketchy,
but early photographs seem to show that the ruined adobe
walls were first removed, and a brick foundation was then
constructed. Walls in the new building were made of adobe,
largely new bricks, but also including fired brick, perhaps
from the ruins of the original building. The Mexican friars
began returning to their own country about 1903, just before
some of the new buildings were ready for occupancy. But
work continued, and the entire 168-foot quadrangle was

[5] Healy, "Father O'Keefe, Rebuilder of Mission San Luis Rey," 19, 23.
Theresa T. Whitcomb, "An Investigation of the Architectural History of
Mission San Luis Rey de Francia," pages unnumbered, unpublished
manuscript in the San Luis Rey Mission archives.

completely enclosed in 1912. The following year the Franciscan Province of the Sacred Heart took charge of San Luis Rey, and in 1915 the Province of Santa Barbara assumed control of the site.[6] The Mexican friars soon regretted their abandonment of the property, but the minister general of the order confirmed title to the Province of Santa Barbara in 1922.[7]

Just at this time, in December 1912, some of the brothers began to work on several parts of the church that had been neglected. The Father Commissary of the Franciscan province

had asked that the Tertiary Chapel (now called the Mortuary Chapel) be restored, and when this work was started, one of the brothers noticed that there was a bricked-up stairway in the east bell-tower. Perhaps not realizing that this had been done while the tower was under construction to make it more resistant to earthquake damage, the friars decided to remove the bricks, and for the first time there was an inside stairway to the choir loft. Restoration of the chapel was

Mortuary Chapel.

---

[6] There is some disagreement about dates of completion. Bishop Cantwell told Father Klumper that the new quadrangle was constructed between 1902 and 1909. See his letter of 6 January 1922, Catholic Diocese of San Diego, archives. Whitcomb says the northwest corner was not completed until the late twenties.

[7] Letter of 23 June 1922, Catholic Diocese of San Diego, archives.

finished in 1914, and it was re-named the Sacred Heart Chapel.[8]

In 1914 the Sisters of the Precious Blood opened a grade school in a temporary building hastily built by Franciscan

The old creamery was added onto the new school.

brothers on land leveled in front of the church. The following year, an old "creamery" building was moved onto the property, tacked onto the original school building, and the whole structure became a four room grade school. Various other buildings were added to the site, probably covering the original majordomo's quarters. In the process of construction the whole field southeast of the mission was filled and leveled. By 1927 enrollment had grown to such an extent, that

[8] San Luis Rey House Chronicle, 1:15-18, Santa Barbara Mission Archive.

an entirely new building was constructed on property purchased just east of the mission. After excavation for foundations, a basement, and various utilities, the property was leveled and landscaped, and the San Luis Rey Boarding School opened here in 1928.[9] Additional ground between the old school and the highway was purchased from the county, presumably after the old road was straightened and moved somewhat to the south.[10]

The various pieces of ground returned to the church in 1865 were separated by a remnant of property known on the U.S. Land Office surveys as Lot No. 7. In order to make the small pieces more useful, Bishop Mora purchased Lot No. 7, some time prior to 1870. Part of Lot No. 7 was included in the San Luis Rey town plat, and this same part was used by Father O'Keefe as a building site for the first clerical quarters. Later, the land became the location for the new grade school. Because of growing concern about having proper land titles, the Franciscans in 1922 exchanged their title to the northeast garden plot (Lot No. 42) for Lot No. 7.[11]

In 1925 the Franciscans decided to transfer the novitiate to San Luis Rey, so major renovations were made in the buildings. In addition, a water reservoir was built on the site of the old mission threshing floor, just northeast of the

[9] Terence Lenhart, "San Luis Rey Mission, 1912 to 1929," unpublished manuscript in the Santa Barbara Mission Archives.

[10] San Luis Rey House Chronicle, 1:23. Lenhart, "San Luis Rey Mission, 1912 to 1929," Santa Barbara Mission Archive.

[11] See the correspondence between Dominic Gallardo and Bishop John J. Cantwell, 24 January 1922 and 11 February 1922, Catholic Diocese of San Diego archives. The transaction is recorded on the "Plat of San Luis Rey Mission Lands" surveyed in June 1923 and filed in the office of the San Diego County Recorder, 11 September 1923, plat map 203.

quadrangle, and the ground east and south of the buildings was leveled for planting. In the middle of the summer the southeast corner of the bell tower collapsed. Much of the

exterior had been plastered during the renovations of 1913-14. Water collecting behind the plaster had weakened the adobe walls. In addition, the lower room of the tower had been packed with adobe after the earthquake of 1812; when these bricks became wet in the heavy rains of 1926, the adobe expanded and forced the wall outward. Reinforced with concrete, the tower was restored the following year.[12]

By the end of 1926 the small quadrangle was enclosed, or nearly so, by a two story building, containing kitchens, living quarters, classrooms, dining areas, and in the main floor of the west wing, a shoe shop, a bakery, a blacksmith shop, and a carpentry shop.[13]The various shops remained here until 1940 and 1941, when they were moved to new buildings northeast of the mission.[14]

Interior of the restored church.

[12] San Luis Rey House Chronicle, 1:15-18, 23-25, Santa Barbara Mission Archive. See also Edith B. Webb's interview of Father Dominic, 30 and 31 December 1937, copy in the Santa Barbara Mission Archives.
[13] "Ground plan of San Luis Rey Mission as in 1922," September 1922, Santa Barbara Mission Archives. Lenhart, "San Luis Rey Mission, 1912-1929," Santa Barbara Mission Archive.
[14] *Provincial Annals: Province of Santa Barbara* (October 1940), 3:44; (April 1941), 3:53.

8

Rebuilding San Luis Rey

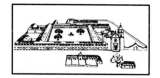

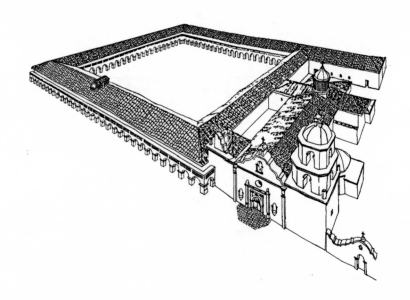

As building progressed around the old mission, the ruined adobe walls were gradually removed from the original quadrangle, and the fragments were used to level the field south of the mission. Around 1929 some of the brothers began excavating the old military barracks and the garden south of the mission, also using this waste to level the field.[1] One of the mission workmen, A. R. Young, discovered a "gargoyle" waterspout in the lower garden in 1931,[2] and for a time a crew was at work excavating a large area. But there was a tragic accident, and

---

[1] Lenhart, "San Luis Rey Mission, 1912 to 1929," Santa Barbara Mission Archive. Oceanside *Blade-Tribune* 10 February 1930, p. 1, typescript in Santa Barbara Mission Archive.

[2] San Diego *Union*, 17 May 1931, p. 1, clipping in San Diego Historical Society. Edith B. Webb discussed this with Cave Couts, Jr., who told her that Father O'Keefe had the garden excavated in 1895; the tile steps, which he said had been about 75 feet wide, were apparently removed at this time. *Indian Life at the Old Missions*, 76-77.

A young friar standing in the ruins of the barracks.

work was abandoned for several years.[3] Excavation of the barracks was resumed in 1937, revealing part of the tile floor. Enough "relics and curios" were recovered to justify renovation of the exhibit rooms in the south wing of the new quadrangle.[4]

Because of increasing enrollment in the seminary, called San Luis Rey College, and perhaps encouraged by a donation from the bishop of San Diego, the Franciscans determined to

[3] Anthony Soto, "Recent Excavations at San Luis Rey Mission: The Sunken Gardens," *Provincial Annals, Province of Santa Barbara, Order of Friars Minor* (April 1960), 22:205-208. This was reprinted with some revisions, the addition of a list of references, and a new title, "Mission San Luis Rey, California—Excavations in the Sunken Gardens," *The Kiva: A Journal of the Arizona Archaeological and Historical Society* (April 1961), 26:34-43.

[4] *Provincial Annals, Province of Santa Barbara* (October 1938), 1:25; (January 1939), 1:30. Webb, *Indian Life at the Old Missions,* 76-77.

The original floor tiles were salvaged for later use.

construct new buildings along the lines of the original quadrangle.[5] Because of work that the brothers had done on the site during the preceding half century, the general layout was well known. For example, the overburden of fallen adobe had been removed from the western colonnades in 1929, revealing the tile floors and the wall fragments and foundations that bordered the interior of the former quadrangle.[6] Subsequent leveling and filling operations uncovered the outer walls on the west and the north. When the contractor was ready to begin work, earthmoving

[5] Letter from Bishop Charles F. Buddy to Matthew Poetzl, 7 October 1949, from Poetzl to Buddy, 8 October 1949, and from Poetzl to Buddy 7 March 1950, Catholic Diocese of San Diego archives.
[6] Lenhart, "San Luis Rey Mission, 1912 to 1929," Santa Barbara Mission Archive.

equipment was used to level the ground about two feet below grade, with the excess dirt spread along the north, the west, and especially the low-lying south side. The remaining arches on the north and west were retained, but the tile floor was removed, the ground excavated, and a concrete walkway placed on the ground. The field just east of the cemetery became the site for mixing adobe bricks. This field was excavated to a depth of three feet to provide materials for adobe bricks. Once construction was finished, the leveled field was covered again with topsoil.[7]

Both this field and the field on the south side of the new west wing were regularly plowed and sowed in alfalfa after 1959. The old school house and land in the south field were purchased from the school board in 1959, allowing the land to be used again for agriculture.[8] A road straightening project had left a small knoll, somewhat obscuring the view between the highway and the mission. This was removed in 1960 by a contractor who needed fill for the trailer park west of the mission property; as part of the project the contractor filled a low area just in front of the driveway entrance.[9]

---

[7] The construction project is well documented in a photograph album at the Santa Barbara Mission Archive. See also the remarks in Maida B. Boyle's "San Luis Rey Mission Report on the Historical and Archaeological Study of Its Primary Construction and Indian Villages Associated with It," pp. 16-17, unpublished MS, March 1968, in San Luis Rey Mission archives. According to Mrs. Boyle, some remnants of foundations and floors on the western side of the quadrangle might still be recoverable under the fill.

[8] San Luis Rey Mission, House Chronicle, 3:112-114.

[9] San Luis Rey Mission, House Chronicle, 3:143-44.

Leveling the ground for the construction of the new
north and west wings, 1949.

Leach lines from the oxidation pool had been installed
earlier in the field between old and new highways 76; these
were extended and deepened in 1963.[10] A swimming pool was
dug on the north side of the mission cemetery in April 1964.
There was additional grading in front of the quadrangle in
1964 and 1965 when the roads and parking lots were paved.[11]

The construction work seemed to have reawakened local
interest in archaeology at San Luis Rey. In the summer of
1955 work was resumed in the south garden. This time there
was an attempt to keep a daily record, with maps, and to

[10] San Luis Rey Mission, House Chronicle, 4:75.
[11] *Provincial Annals, Province of Santa Barbara, Order of Friars Minor*
(April 1964), 26:135; (May 1965), 27:95-96; (June 1965), 27:162. San
Luis Rey Mission, House Chronicle, 4:143.

catalog materials as they were recovered. The site was also listed with the archaeological survey office at UCLA and given the trinomial designation SDi 241; however, no official records are available from this initial research project,[12] although the project supervisor, Anthony Soto published several articles describing the general results of the work.[13] In order to make the site more attractive to visitors, the stairway, removed in 1895, was reinstalled, and some water basins were reconstructed at the foot of the stairs.[14]

However, there has not been a full awareness of the cultural importance of this garden. During the last two decades Highway 76 was relocated, cutting a swath completely through the southern part of the garden and creating a "detention pond" in the garden area south of the road.[15] Cut to a depth of twenty feet or so, this southern tip is now completely sterile, and there is no way to estimate the damage done by this relocation project. Even now the area is

[12] Aside from the 1968 report by Boyle, there are no records of the work performed. An undated letter, probably about January 1968, from Maida B. Boyle to Valentine Healy indicates that photographic files, excavation book, maps, and other, materials were then in Boyle's possession. See the letter and Boyle report, "San Luis Rey Mission Report,", p. 13, San Luis Rey Mission archives.

[13] Published in *Provincial Annals* (April 1960), 22:204-210; *The Kiva* (April 1961), 26:34-43; and an article by Frank L. Graham, based on an interview with Father Soto, "Uncovering the Past at Mission San Luis Rey," *Westways* (May 1958), 50:7.

[14] San Luis Rey Mission, House Chronicle, 3:125, 146; 4:18.

[15] It is unclear whether this "detention pond" was planned in advance or whether it is just an attempt to make the best of a bad decision. See the "Mission San Luis Rey Historic Area: Development Program & Design Guidelines," report prepared for the City of Oceanside by The Planning Center, Newport Beach, CA, 1986.

not safe. Although the "Final Draft" plan made in the 1980s shows new construction safely skirting the "Historic Core," other plans envision a new highway cutting directly across the grounds of San Luis Rey Academy (possible Indian village site) and a new parking lot in the western and southern parts of the lower garden.

Even the mission grounds have not been free from intrusion. In 1959-60 and again in 1984-85 members of a treasure hunting association have dug in the mission compound and gardens, removing important artifacts without due regard for appropriate archaeological protection for the site.[16]

A new school had been built in 1928 on ground east of the mission. This was greatly enlarged in 1948 and enlarged again with the construction of a new chapel in 1955. Between 1957 and 1959 the entrance to the school was relocated, and a circular drive was installed, leading from highway 76 to the new front door. The front of the building was newly landscaped at this time. One of the original school buildings was moved to the north side of the property and converted to use as a laundry.[17]

Almost from the day the mission was abandoned, some people argued that it was a cultural treasure and deserved a better fate. Early visitors were nearly universal in expressing

[16] "Profile of a Treasure Hunter: George Mroczkowski," *Treasure* (April 1973), 4:30-33. Bob Grant, "Found: More Clues to the Mission Treasure," *Treasure Found!" (Summer 1985), 11:20-23, 53.*

[17] *Academy of the Little Flower, San Luis Rey, California, Conducted by the Sisters of the Precious Blood, Formerly San Luis Rey Mission School, San Luis Rey Boarding School: History of Fifty Years, 1913-1963* [San Luis Rey, 1963], pp. 12, 16, 28-29, 33, 36, and 38. See also Stokes, *Franciscan Province of Santa Barbara, 1915-1965,* 37.

this opinion, and the Franciscans who reoccupied the site in 1892 made a real attempt to conserve the historical nature of the site. The study by Duflot de Mofras was perhaps the earliest attempt to present a true architectural view of the buildings, but it was badly flawed. In 1916 Rexford Newcomb published the first professional assessment of the architectural features of this and other mission buildings.[18]

In more recent years various federal and state agencies joined in the preservation effort. The Historic American Buildings Survey recorded the architectural features of the church building during the thirties,[19] and at the same time the State of California placed the mission on the Landmark Register.[20]Finally, the entire mission site, 62.67 acres, was entered on the National Register of Historic Places.[21]

Several recent archaeological studies have been undertaken on land included in the San Luis Rey Mission complex. Excavation and historical research performed by the Westec

[18] Rexford Newcomb, *The Franciscan Mission Architecture of Alta California* (New York: Architectural Book Publishing Co., 1916), plates 26-30.

[19] San Luis Rey de Francia, Historic American Buildings Survey, WPA Project 265-6907, Survey No. Cal. 42. Copies of these records are available in numerous places, including the Oceanside City Planning Department.

[20] Register No. 239, 10 June 1936. California, Division of Beaches and Parks, *California Historical Landmarks* (Sacramento: Office of State Printing, 1970), 47.

[21] But somehow the mission was omitted from the checklist of historic buildings compiled by Alicia Stamm for the Historic American Buildings Survey/Historic American Engineering Record Division of the National Park Service. See *Historic America: Buildings, Structures, and Sites Recorded by the Historic American Buildings Survey and the Historic American Engineering Record,* (Washington: Library of Congress, 1983).

Services Company in 1984 and 1985 established the location of two portions of garden wall and a well or cistern from the garden northeast of the mission.[22] The well is very possibly one of those reopened in 1915 and described by Father Engelhardt in his diary.[23] Duhaut-Cilly said the water was pumped from these wells with a scoop wheel, operated by two men.[24]

Other studies were made for the relocation and widening projects on present Highway 76. One, in 1978, by Greenwood and Associates identified a section of the adobe wall that once divided the south garden. Another study made in 1989 by Debra A. Dominici studied the area in front of San Luis Rey Academy, just north of Highway 76.[25] These and other research projects found the usual scattered evidence of mission-Indian-settler occupation, though no important findings have been published.[26]

[22] Richard Carrico and Terri Jacques, "Mission Wells Project Site: Appendices," appendix B, pp. 2-1 to 2-4, report prepared by Westec Services, Inc., San Diego, for Berry Development Co., Dana Point, CA, 1985. The well is designated SDi-10,078H. The wall sections are designated SDi-10,079H.

[23] Maynard Geiger (ed.), "Diary of the Rev. Zephyrin Engelhardt, O.F.M," *Provincial Annals* (October 1944), 6:61.

[24] Duhaut-Cilly, *Voyage autour du Monde*, 53-54.

[25] Debra A. Dominici, "Archaeological Survey Report for the Highway 76 Widening and New Alignment Project, San Diego County, 11-SD-76," report for the California Department of Transportation, 1989.

[26] D. Sean Cardenas, "Cultural Resource Survey for the Oceanside Emergency Housing Shelter," Report prepared by DSC Environmental Consulting, San Diego, 1989. Richard L. Carrico and Randy L. Franklin, "Cultural Resource Test Sampling Program for a Proposed Flood Control Project in the Lower San Luis Rey River Drainage, Oceanside, California," Report prepared for the U.S. Army Corps of Engineers, Los

(continued...)

Franciscan brothers rebuilding the new mission quadrangle, about 1900-1910.

[26](...continued)
Angeles, by Westec Services, Inc., San Diego, 1979. Sue Ann Cupples and Ken Hedges, "San Luis Rey River Basin: Overview of Cultural Resources," Report prepared for the U.S. Army Corps of "Engineers, Los Angeles, by San Diego State University, 1977. Russell L. Kaldenberg, "An Archaeological Survey of Proposed New Alignment of Route 76 near Mission San Luis Rey de Francia," Report prepared for California Department of Transportation by San Diego State University, 1973. Other reports by Judy Tordoff, Michael Moratto, and Greenwood and Associates describe work at half a dozen sites on or near the mission grounds.

9

San Luis Rey Mission Today

P rior to the arrival of men who made written records the mission grounds were the location for permanent Indian villages. Since 1798 immense structures have been built, looted, destroyed, plowed, dug, graded, and rebuilt with almost total abandon. There are few parts of the original edifices remaining today, except for portions of the church, some parts of the mission colonnades, a few fragments of adobe walls, and some scattered works in brick and tile. Doubtless there are other remnants, but where and what are unknown. One of the most important historical-archaeological sites in California, it has not attracted a great deal of scholarly interest. Most of the studies in a rather considerable list of historical-archaeological research materials, are preliminary or superficial. There has never been a thorough and painstaking investigation of the mission site. Before any additional construction work is done in this area, there should be a complete historical-archaeological study of the grounds, followed by the preparation of a comprehensive plan to conserve the remnants of the record of human activity at Mission San Luis Rey.

All of this is standard practice for historical sites. With sufficient public interest and support, these places can be preserved for the enjoyment and edification of future generations.

A related development that some readers may have noticed is the recent appearance of books and public statements belittling the selfless work and dedication of the Franciscan missionaries, and disparaging the sincerity of their equally fervent Indian converts. Most of the criticisms spring fully developed from the fertile minds of the authors.

Even so, there are dependable modern sources that interested readers will find in local bookstores and libraries. Perhaps the most prolific author is Francis Weber, who has written at least two dozen books on the California missions. The work of Iris Engstrand of the University of San Diego is equally authoritative and readable. Some of the books by these authors are listed in the bibliography, but there are many others, including illustrated volumes by Martin J. Morgado, Norman Neuerburg, and Joel Sweimler.

10
Appendix

Glossary

adobe: an unfired, sun-dried brick
alcalde: an official with civil and judicial authority

Chinigchinich: the religion of the Luisenos before
      conversion to Christianity

friar: a religious brother
fray: title of a Franciscan brother

huerta: a vegetable garden

Luiseños: the people of San Luis Rey village

majordomo: manager
mission: a religious center for conversion of the
      local people; secondarily, a center for
      education and training

neophytes: new converts to Christianity
naranja: orange

potrero: pasture

pueblo: a town

reloj: clock

terrado: flat earthen roof

vara: unit of measurement roughly equivalent to a
     yard
viga: roof beam

Illustration Credits

Cover. Powell Collection, box 20. Huntington Library.

Back cover, bottom. Ford, *Etchings of the Franciscan Missions.* www.lacma.org.

Frontispiece. Powell Collection, box 20, Huntington Library.

Pages xvii & xviii. Engelhardt, *San Luis Rey Mission.*

Page 1. Ford, *Etchings of the Franciscan Missions.*

Page 2. Vischer, *Missions of Upper California.* Digitally reproduced by the USC Digital Library; from the California Historical Society Collection at the University of Southern California.

Page 4. Jones land claim file, Bancroft Library, copy in San Luis Rey mission archives.

Page 10. Tac ms, microfilm, Huntington Library.

Page 17. Harrington, "New Original Version."

Page 18. Robinson, *Life in California.*

Page 24. Robinson, *Life in California*; and Madrid, Spain, Museo Naval.

Page 26. Hutton, William R. *California, 1847-1852.*

Page 30. Powell journal, Bancroft Library, copy in SLR mission archives.

Page 31. Duflot der Mofras, *Exploration du Territoire de L'Oregon.*

Page 35. Duhaut-Cilly, *Voyage autour du Monde. Atlas.*

Page 37. Engelhardt, *San Luis Rey Mission.*

Page 40. *Ibid.*

Page 42. Tac ms, microfilm, Huntington Library.

Page 45. Powell journal, Bancroft Library, copy in SLR archives.

Page 49. SLR mission archives and HABS.

Page 50. HABS.

Page 51. HABS.

Page 57. Tac ms, microfilm, Huntington Library.

Page 58. Powell journal, Bancroft Library, copy in SLR mission archives.

Page 62. Robinson, *Life in California.*

Page 63. Vischer, *Missions of Upper California.*

Page 76. SLR mission archives.

Page 78. Wentworth diary, Bancroft Library, copy in SLR mission archives.

Page 79. Engelhardt, *San Luis Rey Mission.*

Page 80. Vischer, *Missions of Upper California.*

Page 83. Archbishop Alemany claim file 425 N.D., Bancroft Library. Copy SLR mission archives.

Page 85. Vischer, *Missions of Upper California.*

Page 87. Miller, *Account of a Tour of the Missions.*

Page 89. San Diego County Recorder, map books.

Page 91. *Century Magazine* (June 1883).

Page 92. *Ibid.*

Page 94. SLR mission archives.

Page 95. SLR mission archives.

Page 96. SLR mission archives.

Page 97. SLR mission archives.

Page 98. SLR mission archives.

Page 99. SLR mission archives.

Page 100. SLR mission archives.

Page 101. SLR mission archives.

Page 103. Santa Barbara mission archives.

Page 104. SLR mission archives.
Page 108. SLR mission archives.
Page 109. SLR mission archives.
Page 111. SLR mission archives.
Page 116. SLR mission archives.

References

Manuscript Collections

Bancroft Library

Archbishop Joseph S. Alemany, Claimant, Mission Lands, U. S. District Court, Northern District of California, 425 N.D.

Archives of California, State Papers, Missions.

Archives of Santa Barbara

Archivo de las Misiones, 1769-1856, MS C-C 4-5, MS C-C 5.

Bancroft, Hubert H. "Personal Observations during a Tour of the Line of Missions of Upper California." Cal. MS E 113.

César, Julio. "Cosas de Indios de California," MS C-D 109.

Crouch, Herbert. "Reminiscences," (1915), p. 19, typed MS C-D 5039.

Foster, Juan. Deposition in the claim of William C. Jones to the San Luis Rey Mission lands, 30 December 1853. U.S. District Court, Southern District of California, 339 SD.

Hartnell, William E. diary, MS C-E 77.

Hayes Journal, "Emigrant Notes," Journal, and "Mission Book." MS C-E 62.

Locke, Wilma L. "In Search of an Asistencia." Unpublished MS, C-I 13.

Powell, H.M.T. Journal. MS C-F 115.

San Luis Rey, inventory of mission property, MS 68/115:4.

Santa Barbara Mission Archives. *Papeles Miscelaneas.* MS C-C 12.

Whitworth, Robert H. Diary. MS 68/91c.

California State Library

Owen C. Coy Collection

Diocese of San Diego

San Luis Rey files.

Huntington Library

Annual Reports, San Luis Rey Mission. Microfilm MS 42.

Cave J. Couts Collection

Tac, Pablo. "Conversión de los San Luiseños de la Alta California." Microfilm MS 255, rolls 3 and 4.

Oceanside City Planning Department

San Luis Rey de Francia. Historic American Buildings Survey. WPA Project 265-6907, Survey No. Cal. 42.

San Diego County Assessor

Map Books

San Diego County Recorder

Map Books

San Diego Historical Society

Crouch, Herbert. Diary, MS 920 CRO.
San Diego County Plat Books.
U. S. Census, San Luis Rey, CA. 1850 (photostat), 1860 (original), and 1870 (photostat).

San Luis Rey Mission Archives

Boyle, Maida B. "San Luis Rey Mission Report on the Historical and Archaeological Study of Its Primary Construction and Indian Villages Associated With It." Unpublished MS, 1968.
Whitcomb, Theresa. "An Investigation of the Architectural History of Mission San Luis Rey de Francia." Unpublished MS, 1983.

Santa Barbara Mission Archives

Cave Couts, Jr. Interview, 1 September 1932. Webb Collection. Vol. XVIII.

Lenhart, Terence. "San Luis Rey Mission, 1912 to 1929." Unpublished MS, 1965.

San Luis Rey, House Chronicle.

Tintle, Kean. "Mission San Luis Rey, 1893-1900." Unpublished MS, 1965.

U.S. Archives, Federal Records Center, Laguna Niguel

California Land Office, Survey Plat Maps. Plat Book 49. Record Group 49.

Books and Periodicals

Academy of the Little Flower, San Luis Rey, California, Conducted Mission School, San Luis Rey Boarding School: History of Fifty Years, 1913-1963. San Luis Rey: n.n., 1963.

Adams, Samuel, to James Warren, 29 October, 1777, Massachusetts Historical Collections, vol. 1 of 2 (Boston: Massachusetts Historical Society, 1917), 375.

Ames, George Walcott, Jr. (ed.). "A Doctor Comes to California: The Diary of John S. Griffin, Assistant Surgeon with Kearny s Dragoons, 1846-47."

California Historical Society Quarterly. (September and December 1942), 21:193-224, 333-57.

Axe, Ruth F., Edwin H. Carpenter, and Norman Neuerburg, *A Visit to the Missions of Southern California in February and March 1874 by Henry Oak.* Los Angeles: Southwest Museum, 1981.

Bancroft, Hubert H. *History of California,* vol. 1, *1542-1800,* and vol. 2, *1801-1824.* San Francisco: The History Co., 1886.

Bannon, John F. *The Spanish Borderlands Frontier, 1513-1821.* New York: Holt, Rinehart & Winston, 1970.

Bartlett, John R. *Personal Narrative of Exploration and Incidents in Texas, New Mexico, California, Sonora, and Chihuahua.* New York: D. Appleton & Co., 1854.

Bean, Lowell J., and Harry Lawton. "Some Explanations for the Rise of Cultural Complexity in Native California with Comments on Proto-Agriculture and Agriculture." *Native Californians: A Theoretical Retrospective.* Edited by Lowell J. Bean and Thomas C. Blackburn. Socorro, N.M.: Ballena Press, 1976.

Bolton, Herbert E. (ed.). *Fray Juan Crespí, Missionary Explorer on the Pacific Coast, 1769-1774.* Berkeley: University of California Press, 1927.

Boscana, Gerónimo, *"Memoria breve de las costumbres gentilicas de los Yndios de San Juan Capistrano."* Henry and Paule Reichlen (eds.). *"Le Manuscrit Boscana de la Bibliothèque Nationale de Paris: Relation sur les Indiens Acâgchemem de la Mission de San Juan Capistrano, Californie."* *Journal de la Société des Américanistes.* (1971), 15:233-73.

California Division of Beaches and Parks, *California Historical Landmarks*. Sacramento: Office of State Printing, 1970.

Cardenas, D. Sean. "Cultural Resource Survey for the Oceanside Emergency Housing Shelter." Report prepared by DSC Environmental Consulting, San Diego, 1989.

Carrico, Richard L., and Randy L. Franklin. "Cultural Resource Test Sampling Program for a Proposed Flood Control Project in the Lower San Luis Rey River Drainage, Oceanside, California." Report prepared for the U.S. Army Corps of Engineers, Los Angeles, by Westec Services, Inc., San Diego, 1979.

Carrico, Richard L., and Terri Jacques. "Mission Wells Project Site: Appendices," Appendix B. Report prepared for Barry Development Co., Dana Point, CA, by Westec Services, Inc., San Diego, 1985.

Carter, Charles F. "Duhaut-Cilly s Account of California in the Years 1827-28." *California Historical Quarterly*. (June 1929), 8:131-65.

César, Julio. "Recollections of My Youth at San Luis Rey Mission: The Memories of a Full-blooded Indian, of Affairs and Events Witnessed at One of California s Most Famous `Cathedrals of the Sun. " Edited by Nellie Van de Grift Sanchez. *Touring Topics*. (November 1930), 22:42-43.

Cook, Sherburne F. *The Population of the California Indians, 1769-1970*. Berkeley: University of California Press, 1976.Cook, Sherburne F., and Woodrow Borah. *Essays in Population History: Mexico and California.*

3 Vols. Berkeley: University of Califomia Press, 1979.

Cruz, Gilbert R. *Let There Be Towns: Spanish Municipal Origins in the American Southwest, 1610-1810.* College Station, TX: Texas A&M University Press, 1988.

Cupples, Sue Ann, and Ken Hedges. "San Luis Rey River Basin: Overview of Cultural Resources." Report prepared for the U.S. Army Corps of Engineers, Los Angeles, by San Diego State University, 1977.

Cutter, Donald F. "The La Jolla, Rincon, Pauma, Pala, and San Pasqual Indian Reservations in Historical Perspective." Report filed in Rincon Band et. al., *v.* Escondido Mutual Water Company et. al., S. D. Cal. No. 69-217-S.

Cybulski, Jerome S. "Possible Pre-Columbian Treponematosis on Santa Rosa Island, California." *Canadian Review of Physical Anthropology.* (Nos. 1 & 2 1980), 2:19-25.

Dominici, Debra A. "Archaeological Survey Report for the Highway 76 Widening and New Alignment Project, San Diego County, 11-SD-76." Report prepared for the California Department of Transportation, 1989.

Doyle, John T. "Introduction," to Francisco Palóu, *Noticias de la Nueva California Escritas por el Rev. Padre Fr. Francisco Palóu.* San Francisco: Imprenta de Edouardo Bosqui & Cia. 1974.

Dubois, Constance G. "The Religion of the Luiseño Indians of Southern California." *University of California Publications in American Archaeology and Ethnology.* (No. 3 1908).

Duflot de Mofras, Eugene. *Exploration du Territoire de L'Orégon, des Californie et de la Mer Vermeille.* 2 vols. in 4. Paris: Arthus Bertrand, 1844.

Duhaut-Cilly, Auguste Bernard. *Voyage autour du Monde Principalmente à la Californie.* 2 vols. Paris: A. Bertrand, 1834-35.

Emory, William H. *Notes of a Military Reconnaissance from Fort Leavenworth, in Missouri, to San Diego in California, including Parts of the Arkansas, Del Norte, and Gila Rivers.* Washington: Wendell & Van Benthuysen Printer, 1848.

Engelhardt, Zephyrin. *San Luis Rey Mission.* San Francisco: James H. Barry Co., 1921.

Engstrand, Iris W. *Serra's San Diego: Father Junípero Serra and California's Beginnings.* San Diego, CA: San Diego Historical Society, c. 1982.

Engstrand, Iris W., and Neuerburg, Norman. *Early California reflections : an exhibit presented at the San Juan Capistrano Regional Branch of Orange County Public Library,* San Juan Capistrano, CA: The Library, c.1986.

Forbes, Alexander. *California: A History of Upper and Lower California.* London: Smith, Elder & Co., 1839.

Ford, Henry C. *Etchings of the Franciscan Missions of California.* New York: Studio Press, 1883.

Geiger, Maynard. (ed.) "Diary of the Rev. Zephyrin Engelhardt, O.F.M." *Provincial Annals.* (October 1944), 6:53-62.

Gentilcore, Rocco L. "Missions and Mission Lands of Alta California." *Annals of the Association of American Geographers.* (March 1961), 51:46-72.

Gifford, Edward W. "Clans and Moieties in Southern California." *University of California Publications in American Archaeology and Ethnology.* (No. 2 1918), 14:155-202.

Graham, Frank L. "Uncovering the Past at Mission San Luis Rey. *Westways.* (May 1958), 50:7.

Grant, Bob. "Found: More Clues to the Mission Treasure." *Treasure Found!* (Summer 1985), 11:20-23,53.

Gunn, Douglas. *San Diego: Climate, Production, Resources, Topography, etc., etc.* 4th ed. rev. San Diego: Union Steam Book and Job Office, 1886.

Gunn, Douglas. *San Diego Illustrated: Climate, Resources, Topography, Productions, etc., etc.* San Diego: San Diego Printing Co., 1887.

Healy, Valentine. "Father O Keefe, Rebuilder of Mission San Luis Rey." *Times Gone By: The Journal of San Diego History.* (June 1965), 11:15-25.

Hedges, Ken. "Hakataya Figurines from Southern California." *Pacific Coast Archæological Society Quarterly.* (No. 3 1973), 9:1-40.

Henige, David. "On the Contact Population of Hispaniola: History as Higher Mathematics." *Hispanic American Historical Review.* (May 1978), 58:217-37.

Hewes, Minna and Gordon. *Indian Life at Mission San Luis Rey.* San Luis Rey, CA: Old Mission, 1958.

Hughes, Charles (ed.). "A Military View of San Diego in 1847." The Journal of San Diego History. (Summer 1974), 20:33-43.

Hutton, William R. *California, 1847-1852.* San Marino: Huntington Library, 1942.

Jackson, Helen H. "Father Junípero and His Work," *The Century Illustrated Monthly Magazine*. (June 1883), 26:199-215.

Jones, Oakah L. *Los Paisanos: Spanish Settlers on the Northern Frontier of New Spain*. Norman: University of Oklahoma Press, 1979.

Kaldenberg, Russell L. "An Archaeological Survey of Proposed New Alignment of Route 76 Near Mission San Luis Rey de Francia." Report prepared for California Department of Transportation by San Diego State University, 1973.

Kelsey, Harry. *Juan Rodríguez Cabrillo*. San Marino, CA: Huntington Library, 1986.

Kelsey, Harry. "European Impact on the California Indians," *The Americas*. (April 1985), 41:494-511.

Kelsey, Harry. "The California Indian Treaty Myth." *Southern California Quarterly*. (Fall 1973), 55:225-238.

Kelsey, Harry. "The Mission Buildings of San Juan Capistrano: A Tentative Chronology." *Southern California Quarterly*. (Spring 1987), 69:1-32.

Kenneally, Finbar. *Writings of Fermín Francisco de Lasuén*. 2 vols. Washington: Academy of American Franciscan History, 1965.

Kenneally, Finbar. "San Luis Rey Golden Jubilee." *Provincial Annals*. (January-April 1955), 17:93-111.

Kloos, Helmut. "Valley Fever (Coccidioidomycosis): Changing Concepts of a `California Disease. " *Southern California Quarterly*. (Spring 1973), 55:59-88.

Koerper, Henry C., and E. Bonita Fouste. "An Interesting Late Prehistoric Burial from CA-ORA-119-A." *Pacific Coast Archaeological Society Quarterly.* (April 1977), 13:39-61.

Lamadrid Jiménez, Lazaro. *El Alaves Fray Fermín Francisco de Lasuén, O.F.M.* (1736-1803). Vitoria: Diputación Foral de Alava, Consejo de Cultura, 1963.

Los Angeles *Star.* 9 October 1869.

Lothrop, Gloria R. "El Viejo: Serra in Context," *The Californians.* (November-December 1989), 7.

McCown, B. E. "Temeku: A Page from the History of the Luiseño Indians." *Papers of the Archaeological Survey Association of Southern California.* (No. 3 1955).

McHenry, Henry. "Transverse Lines in Long Bones of Prehistoric California Indians." *American Journal of Physical Anthropology.* (July 1968), 29:1-18.

Meighan, Clement W. "Indians and California Missions." *Southern California Quarterly.* (Fall 1987), 49:187-201.

Melbourne, Robert E. "San Luis Rey in the Nineteenth Century: Its People, Institutions and Events." Master s thesis, University of San Diego, 1990.

Merbs, Charles F. "Patterns of Health and Sickness in the Precontact Southwest." David H. Thomas (ed.). Columbian Consequences: *Archaeological and Historical Perspectives on the Spanish Borderlands West.* Washington: Smithsonian Institution Press, 1989.

Miller, Henry. *Account of a Tour of the California Missions, 1856.* San Francisco: Book Club of California, 1952.

"Mission San Luis Rey Historic Area: Development Program & Design Guidelines." Report prepared for the City of Oceanside by the Planning Center, Newport Beach, CA, 1986.

Moratto, Michael J. *California Archaeology*. Orlando, FL: Academic Press, Inc., 1984.

Morgado, Martin J. *Junípero Serra: A Pictorial Biography* (Monterey, CA: Siempre adelante Publishing, 1991).

Morrison, Harry B. "The Archbishop s Claim: The History of the Legal Claim of the Catholic Church before the Federal Courts to the Property of the California Missions." *The Jurist*. (No. 2 1987), 47:394-422.

Neuerburg, Norman. *The Decoration of the California Missions* (Santa Barbara, CA: Bellerphon Books, 1987).

Newcomb, Rexford. *The Franciscan Mission Architecture of Alta California*. New York: Architectural Book Publishing Co., 1916.

Oceanside *Blade*. 1 January 1898.

Oceanside *Blade-Tribune*. 10 February 1930.

"Profile of a Treasure Hunter: George Mroczkowski." *Treasure*. (April 1973), 4:30-33.

Ritter, Eric, and Peter D. Schulz. "Mortuary Practices and Health Conditions among a Small Prehistoric Population from Baja California Sur." *Pacific Coast Archaeological Society Quarterly*. (January 1975), 11:43-53.

Sacramento *Daily Alta California*. 24 November 1868.

Salls, Roy. "Skeletal Remains from the Ripper s Cove Site, Santa Catalina Island, California." *Pacific Coast*

Archaeological Society Quarterly. (1984), 20:26-27.
San Diego Union. 17 May 1931.

Scharf, Thomas L. "Pages from the Diary of Cave Johnson
Couts: San Diego in the Summer of 1849. *Journal of
San Diego History.* (Spring 1976), 22:9-19.

Soto, Anthony. "Recent Excavations at San Luis Rey
Mission: The Sunken Gardens." *Provincial Annals,
Province of Santa Barbara, Order of Friars Minor.*
(April 1960), 22:205-208.

Soto, Anthony. "Mission San Luis Rey,
California—Excavations in the Sunken Gardens." The
*Kiva: A Journal of the Arizona Archaeological and
Historical Society.* (April 1961), 26:34-43.

Stamm, Alice. *Historic America: Buildings, Structures, and
Sites Recorded by the Historic American Buildings
Survey and the Historic American Engineering
Record.* Washington: Library of Congress, 1983.

Stokes, Bernard H. *Franciscan Province of Santa Barbara,
1915-1965.* Santa Barbara: Santa Barbara Mission,
Serra Press, 1965.

Strong, William D. "Aboriginal Society in Southern
California." *University of California Publications in
American Archaeology and Ethnology.* ((No. 1 1929),
26:1-358.

*Sweimler, Joel. Mission San Luis Rey. Boston: Colour-
picture Publishers, c. 1992).*

Tac, Pablo. *"Conversión de los San Luiseños de la Alta
California."* Edited by Carlo Tagliavini in
*"Lévangelizzazione e i Costumi degli Indi Luiseños
secondo la Narrazione di un Chierico Indigeno."*

Proceedings of the Twenty-third International Congress of Americanists. (1930), 633-48.

Tibesar, Antonine (ed.). *Junípero Serra and the Northwest Mexican Frontier, 1750-1825.* Washington, DC: Academy of American Franciscan History, 1985.

Transactions of the California State Agricultural Society during the Year 1858. Sacramento: John O Meara, State Printer, 1859.

True, Delbert L., Clement W. Meighan, and Harvey Crew. "Archaeological Investigations at Molpa, San Diego County, California." *University of California Publications in Anthropology.* (1974), 11.

True, Delbert L. "An Early Complex in San Diego County." *American Antiquity.* (January 1958), 23.

True, Delbert L. "Archaeological Sites in San Diego County, California: Preliminary Report on Sites SDi-4558, 4562, and 4562A." Report to the California Department of Transportation, 1977.

True, Delbert L. "The Pauma Complex in Northern San Diego County: 1978." *Journal of New World Archaeology.* (No. 4 1980), 3.

Vancouver, George. *A Voyage of Discovery to the North Pacific Ocean and Round the World, 1791-1795.* Edited by W. Kaye Lamb. 4 vols. London: Hakluyt Society, 1984.

Vischer, Edward. *Drawings of the California Missions, 1861-1878.* San Francisco: Book Club of California, 1982.

Vischer, Edward. *Missions of Upper California, 1872.* San Francisco: Winterburn & Co., 1872.

Walker, Phillip L., Patricia Lambert, and Michael J. DeNiro. "The Effects of European Contact on the Health of

Alta California Indians." David H. Thomas (ed.). *Columbian Consequences: Archaeological and Historical Perspectives on the Spanish Borderlands West.* Washington: Smithsonian Institution Press,1989.

Wagner, Henry R. *Spanish Voyages to the Northwest Coast of America in the Sixteenth Century.* (San Francisco: California Historical Society, 1929).

Webb, Edith B. *Indian Life at the Old Missions.* Los Angeles: Warren F. Lewis Publ., 1952.

Weber, Francis J. *Francis Mora, Last of the Catalans.* Los Angeles: Westernlore Press, 1967.

Weber, Francis J. *Joseph Sadoc Alemany, Harbinger of a New Era.* Los Angeles: Dawson s Book Shop, 1973.

White, Raymond C. "Luiseño Social Organization." *University of California Publications in American Archaeology and Ethnology.* (No. 2 1963), 48:91-194.

Index

A

Agua Hedionda 44.
Alemany, Joseph S. 49, 78
All Saints Cemetery 86. *See also* cemeteries.
Amat, Thaddeus 82.

B

Bancroft, Hubert H. 48, 50, 80-85.
Bancroft, Kate 85.
Bartlett, John R. 80-81.
Bidwell, John 73.
Boscana, Gerónimo 16-18.
Buena Vista 44-45.
buildings 35-37, 50-55, 91-99, 105-110.
Baptismal font 49.

C

Cabrillo, Juan Rodríguez 3, 11, 14.
Cantwell, John J. 95-97.
cemeteries 78, 80, 86. *See also* All Saints Cemetery; Pioneer Cemetery.

Cermeño, Sebastián Rodriguez 14.
César, Julio 45, 64, 67.
Chinigchinich 16, 17, 44.
church 35, 36, 52-53, 73-74, 78, 80, 82, 85.
Cleal, John G. 49, 79, 81.
clock 54, 56.
clothes 57.
Cook, Sherburne F, 42-43.
Cot, Antonio José, 66.
courtyard 47, 54, 92. *See also* buildings.
crafts 33, 47-48, 92.
Crespí, Juan 27, 29.

D

Daily Alta California 76.
deaths 72.
Del Mar 11.
disease 21, 67-68.
Dominici, Debra 111.
Duell, Prentice 57.
Duhaut-Cilly 32, 36, 49, 51, 56, 111.

CPSIA information can be obtained
at www.ICGtesting.com
Printed in the USA
FSOW02n0540020616
21046FS